"I don't know if I've ever read a book on prayer that left me feeling the entire range of human emotion—until reading John Onwuchekwa's *Prayer*. Here is a human book—beautiful, poignant, funny, gritty, and pastoral. This book is better than a correction to our often languid prayer lives. There's no guilt-based manipulation. Onwuchekwa writes like a fellow traveler, and as a fellow traveler knows what travelers need most: refreshment. Here's a thirst-quenching encouragement to join together in seeking our great God. I pray every church reads *Prayer* together; it will change our congregations. Here's a warm invitation to the entire church, beckoning the people of God to the wonders of prayer."

Thabiti Anyabwile, Pastor, Anacostia River Church, Washington, DC; author, *What Is a Healthy Church Member?*

"*Prayer* is an excellent book by my dear friend John Onwuchekwa. It is biblically and theologically rich. It is also real and honest. Want to get a corporate prayer meeting started in your church? This book is a very good start."

Daniel L. Akin, President, Southeastern Baptist Theological Seminary

"Everyone remembers that auntie or uncle who hushed our fears with the words, 'Baby, we just gon' pray on that.' John Onwuchekwa is that voice for today, calling the church back to one of the simplest and most powerful tools in her arsenal—the habit of communal prayer. He doesn't merely want to reawaken our atrophied prayer muscles; he invites us into the much harder work of reorienting our priorities so that they're more in line with God's. Onwuchekwa's call to return to such 'first things' is an excellent start to seeing Christian communities moving in the same kingdom direction."

K. A. Ellis, Cannada Fellow for World Christianity, Reformed Theological Seminary

"There's likely something missing in your church, something you haven't thought much of and likely haven't even noticed. It's prayer. Onwuchekwa shares compelling, insightful, and biblical reasons why corporate prayer should be a priority for the church. What a privilege it is to pray together as a family—this is the vision Onwuchekwa casts for us. This book has the potential to transform not only individuals, but also our relationships and the culture in our churches. I highly recommend it."

Trillia Newbell, author, *God's Very Good Idea*; *Enjoy*; and *Fear and Faith*

"The early church moved forward in power because they were a praying church (Acts 4:31). If we today are so proficient at ministry mechanics that we can succeed without power from on high, we have failed. But if our churches today will heed this compelling call to prayer by John Onwuchekwa, we too will prevail against all earthly powers, for God's glory!"

Ray Ortlund, Lead Pastor, Immanuel Church, Nashville, Tennessee

"This is a thought-provoking book about the life of prayer in the local church. Onwuchekwa builds a theological framework and then gives tangible and practical solutions for fleshing it out. I've had the privilege of working with John over the last decade, and I've seen no one better able to take lofty concepts and present them in a way that is palatable for the body of Christ. This book is an outworking of his gift. He takes biblical principles and communicates them in an effective way. His work on this subject is a gift to the church."

Dhati Lewis, Lead Pastor, Blueprint Church, Atlanta, Georgia; Executive Director of Community Restoration, North American Mission Board; author, *Among Wolves: Disciple-Making in the City*

"What more could be needed by our churches than a revival of gospel-centered spirituality? And what more could we do to experience this revival than to recommit to nourishing communion with our Father through prayer? This is why I'm thankful for this exceptional book by John Onwuchekwa. It is an accessible, practical, and relatable guide to the depths of the enormous, glorious privilege of speaking to the God of the universe."

Jared C. Wilson, Director of Content Strategy, Midwestern Baptist Theological Seminary; Director, Pastoral Training Center, Liberty Baptist Church, Kansas City, Missouri; author, *Supernatural Power for Everyday People*

"I have a lot to say about this little book, because it's so good. In fact, I think this is one of the best books in this series. Brief and well written, this book by pastor John Onwuchekwa looks especially at two sections of the Gospels—the Lord's Prayer and Jesus's prayer in the garden of Gethsemane. Onwuchekwa shares significant observations that seem intuitive, but are also surprising. It is well illustrated, biblically faithful, and theologically accurate. This book is useful to think not only about when we should pray, but also about how we should pray, and even what we should pray about. It reintroduces us to the ignored topic of praying together at church. Hope-giving and inspiring, specific and practical, the whole book is sweetened by touches of humor. You and others could benefit from investing your time in reading this small book on such a grand topic."

Mark Dever, Senior Pastor, Capitol Hill Baptist Church, Washington, DC; President, 9Marks

PRAYER

9Marks: Building Healthy Churches

Edited by Mark Dever and Jonathan Leeman

Church Discipline: How the Church Protects the Name of Jesus, Jonathan Leeman

Church Membership: How the World Knows Who Represents Jesus, Jonathan Leeman

Sound Doctrine: How a Church Grows in the Love and Holiness of God, Bobby Jamieson

Church Elders: How to Shepherd God's People Like Jesus, Jeramie Rinne

Evangelism: How the Whole Church Speaks of Jesus, Mack Stiles

Expositional Preaching: How We Speak God's Word Today, David Helm

The Gospel: How the Church Portrays the Beauty of Christ, Ray Ortlund

Discipling: How to Help Others Follow Jesus, Mark Dever

Conversion: How God Creates a People, Michael Lawrence

Missions: How the Local Church Goes Global, Andy Johnson

Biblical Theology: How the Church Faithfully Teaches the Gospel, Nick Roark and Robert Cline

Prayer: How Praying Together Shapges the Church, John Onwuchekwa

BUILDING HEALTHY CHURCHES

PRAYER

HOW
PRAYING
TOGETHER
SHAPES THE
CHURCH

JOHN ONWUCHEKWA

CROSSWAY®

WHEATON, ILLINOIS

Cover design: Darren Welch

First printing 2018

Printed in the United States of America

Hardcover ISBN: 978-1-4335-5947-1
ePub ISBN: 978-1-4335- 5950-1
PDF ISBN: 978-1-4335-5948-8
Mobipocket ISBN: 978-1-4335-5949-5

Library of Congress Cataloging-in-Publication Data

Names: Onwuchekwa, John, author.
Title: Prayer : how praying together shapes the church / John Onwuchekwa.
Description: Wheaton : Crossway, 2018. | Series: 9Marks: building healthy churches | Includes bibliographical references and index.
Identifiers: LCCN 2018003481 (print) | LCCN 2018024421 (ebook) | ISBN 9781433559488 (pdf) | ISBN 9781433559495 (mobi) | ISBN 9781433559501 (epub) | ISBN 9781433559471 (hc)
Subjects: LCSH: Prayer—Christianity.
Classification: LCC BV210.3 (ebook) | LCC BV210.3 .O67 2018 (print) | DDC 248.3/2—dc23
LC record available at https://lccn.loc.gov/2018003481

Crossway is a publishing ministry of Good News Publishers.

LB		29	28	27	26	25	24	23	22	21	20		
15	14	13	12	11	10	9	8	7	6	5	4	3	

To my mom, who taught me to pray.
To my dad, who modeled the courage that came from prayer.
To my wife, Shawndra, my lifelong prayer partner.
To Ava, you are the ripened fruit after a
long season of prayers sown.
To Cornerstone Church, your faith and
love have increased mine.

CONTENTS

SERIES PREFACE

The 9Marks series of books is premised on two basic ideas. First, the local church is far more important to the Christian life than many Christians today perhaps realize.

Second, local churches grow in life and vitality as they organize their lives around God's Word. God speaks. Churches should listen and follow. It's that simple. When a church listens and follows, it begins to look like the One it is following. It reflects his love and holiness. It displays his glory. A church will look like him as it listens to him.

So our basic message to churches is, don't look to the best business practices or the latest styles; look to God. Start by listening to God's Word again.

Out of this overall project comes the 9Marks series of books. Some target pastors. Some target church members. Hopefully all will combine careful biblical examination, theological reflection, cultural consideration, corporate application, and even a bit of individual exhortation. The best Christian books are always both theological and practical.

It's our prayer that God will use this volume and the others to help prepare his bride, the church, with radiance and splendor for the day of his coming.

INTRODUCTION

If you were to walk into most churches next Sunday, what would you find?

You would hear music and singing. It might be loud or sparse, the songs new or old. Yet the basic structure would be almost identical whether you were in Billings, Montana, or Atlanta, Georgia.

There would be some sort of sermon. It might be topical, brief, and generally lighthearted. Or it might be expositional, long, and generally serious. Depending on the Sunday, you might see a baptism, participate in the Lord's Supper, or engage in a corporate Scripture reading.

But you know what you probably wouldn't see a lot of? Or participate in?

Prayer.

I don't mean that no one will talk to God. But the prayers will likely be brief and few, a couple of cursory words as musicians and speakers shuffle on and off stage. They will likely be biblical but vague, focusing on the general promises of God for an undefined subset of people. They will likely be informative but territorial, rarely going beyond the immediate needs of those within earshot. They will likely be emotionally intense, springing forth from the hearts of people who really do have an earnest desire to communicate with their God.

The thing is, the prayers won't slow down and linger on the glories of God, his attributes, and his character. They won't meditate unhurriedly on his Word. They won't ask hearers to study their own hearts and confess specific sins. They won't ask God for help to do what only he can do: save the lost, feed the hungry, liberate captives, give wisdom to world leaders, fix broken institutions, sustain persecuted Christians.

This is a problem—and it seems many churches simply don't realize how little they pray together, or how little their prayers reflect the bigheartedness of God. I'm reminded of John Stott's description of a prayer service he once visited. Does it sound familiar to you?

> I remember some years ago visiting a church incognito. I sat in the back row. . . . When we came to the pastoral prayer, it was led by a lay brother, because the pastor was on holiday. So he prayed that the pastor might have a good holiday. Well, that's fine. Pastors should have good holidays. Second, he prayed for a lady member of the church who was about to give birth to a child that she might have a safe delivery, which is fine. Third, he prayed for another lady who was sick, and then it was over. That's all there was. It took twenty seconds. I said to myself, it's a village church with a village God. They have no interest in the world outside. There was no thinking about the poor, the oppressed, the refugees, the places of violence, and world evangelization.[1]

What Stott describes here is likely true for so many churches: village prayers to village gods.

I've heard Mark Dever say that we should pray so much in our church gatherings that the nonbelievers get bored. We talk too much to a God they don't believe in.

Maybe that's hyperbole, but certainly we—by which I mean we as Christians and church members *together*—should pray bigger and better and more biblical prayers.

In a sentence, that's the goal of this book: learning how to pray better and more as churches. Just as our private prayer lives can be improved by God's grace, so too can our corporate prayer lives.

THE ROAD AHEAD

No single book on prayer can say everything that needs to be said about prayer. Plus, a fruitful prayer life is cultivated by constant practice, not the comprehension of propositions. Yet as we take this journey together, I want to make sure that you're aware of my intended destination. My hope is that this book will be a guide and a springboard that helps you enjoy the amazing gift of prayer we have *as a church*.

Of all the books that have been written on prayer, this one has a very specific purpose: examining how prayer shapes the life of the church. So much has been written about prayer as an individual discipline. Not much has been written about prayer as a necessary and communal activity that shapes local churches, either by its presence or absence (though Megan Hill's *Praying Together* is helpful [Crossway, 2016]).

Think of this book as offering a few crucial puzzle pieces that were missing from an already assembled, five-hundred-piece puzzle on prayer. I'm the beneficiary of others who have done the hard work of assembling most of the picture.

Let me give you a preview of what we'll cover in this book. Chapter 1 will present our problem: corporate prayerlessness. Chapter 2 offers a road to a solution. We'll take some time understanding what we mean by *prayer* so that we can move forward together.

Chapters 3 and 4 examine how Jesus talked about prayer, which offers us a template. Chapter 5 moves from propositional truths about prayer to examining Jesus's powerful practice of prayer in the midst of crisis.

The last part of the book, chapters 6–8, will be more practical. Having established the benefits of corporate prayer and how it shapes the church, these chapters will discuss how to incorporate prayer into the life of a church. We'll address various topics: prayer in corporate worship, prayer meetings, and how corporate prayer shapes both our corporate mission and our pursuit of diversity.

May you take this book for what it's worth, and may your church flourish through robust and regular corporate prayer.

1

BREATHE AGAIN

The Problem of Prayerlessness

PRAYER IS BREATHING

Well, here you are reading another book on prayer. Maybe the last one didn't make you feel guilty enough, and you're a glutton for punishment. What good is a book on prayer without an initial quote that surfaces your shortcomings as a pray-er? Without further ado, here it goes: "To be a Christian without prayer is no more possible than to be alive without breathing!"[1]

All jokes aside, that may be the most potent and challenging statement on prayer I've ever read. Breathing—as a metaphor for Christian prayer—captures so much of what prayer should be. It reminds us that prayer is something essential to our existence. Breathing is necessary for everything we do. It enables every activity. Likewise, prayer is basic and vital. It's tied to both our present existence and perpetual endurance. Prayer is breathing. There's no better metaphor of what prayer should be for the Christian.

That's why the struggle many Christians have with prayer is so puzzling. Isn't it strange how so many Christians believe this truth in principle, but so few churches ratify it in practice?

Our problem isn't the way we talk about prayer. We talk about it with all the fervency and eloquence it deserves. Our problem is the way we treat prayer. Our practice doesn't line up with our proclamations, which is always a sign that something is off (see James 2).

A total absence of prayer in the church isn't a likely problem. Maybe a church somewhere out there never prays at all, but I don't assume that's happening in yours. I don't know your church, but I bet there are times you come together to pray. Such praying may be sparse and sporadic, but it happens.

And therein lies what I think is the biggest problem: not a complete lack of prayer, but too little prayer. Here's another quote to surface more of those prayer-related insecurities: "So we come to one of the crying evils of these times, maybe of all times—little or no praying. Of these two evils, perhaps little praying is worse than no praying. Little praying is a kind of make-believe, a salvo for the conscience, a farce and a delusion. The little estimate we put on prayer is evident from the little time we give to it."[2]

When prayer is sparse and sporadic, when it's done just enough to ease the conscience and not much more, we've got a problem. We've all been a part of churches where prayer is present but neither purposeful nor potent. Unfortunately, our prayers in the church too often feel like prayer before a meal: obligatory and respectable, but no one really gets much out of it. Our church prayers get reduced to a tool for transitioning from one activity to the next. Let's have everyone close their eyes and bow their heads, so that transitioning the praise team on and off the stage isn't so awkward.

Do you see the danger in too little prayer? Where prayer is present, it's saying something—it's speaking, shouting. It teaches the church that we *really* need the Lord. Where prayer is absent, it reinforces the assumption that we're okay without him. Infrequent prayer teaches a church that God is needed only in special situations—under certain circumstances but not all. It teaches a church that God's help is intermittently necessary, not consistently so. It leads a church to believe that there are plenty of things we can do without God's help, and we need to bother him only when we run into especially difficult situations.

Reflect with me for a moment about the racially inflammatory events that bombarded the United States during the summer of 2016. In one week our nation witnessed the deaths of Philando Castile, Alton Sterling, and five police officers in Dallas. People took sides, and every side had something to mourn. It was against this backdrop that many churches gathered corporately to pray for their communities, churches, leaders, and nation. Some churches gathered with churches across denominational lines. For a season, our prayers seemed potent, pressing, and purposeful. It was our screaming out, "God, we need your help!"

Once these crises had passed, however, corporate praying like this all but ceased. That's telling, isn't it? It reveals that we treat prayer as something special, meant to take care of things that we can't "handle" on our own. We don't treat prayer like breathing. We treat it like prescription medication meant to rid us of an infection. Once the infection is gone, so is the frequency and fervency of our prayers.

A MOMENT OF HONESTY

Allow me to be brutally honest for a minute. Since I don't have to look any of you in the eye, I feel a bit more courageous in admitting my faults. If you're anything like me, and reading a book on prayer makes you feel like a failure, then please know that writing a book on prayer makes me feel like a hypocrite. I'll be the first to admit that I'm no expert when it comes to prayer. I don't feel particularly proficient at it. I wouldn't put "mighty man of prayer" on my résumé. I struggle with prayer. I always have. I feel like my prayers are often weak.

I say this because I've seen people who are mighty prayers, and I know I'm not one of them. My mom is. I remember watching her come home from work every day and greet us briefly en route to her room. On those days when her bedroom door was cracked, I would squint through the opening and see her get on her knees by her bed to pray. She emerged a different person. She did this *every day*. To this very day, she won't let me off of a phone call until she prays for me. And if she forgets, she calls back and leaves a voice mail. My dad was the same way. So when they planted a church in 2001, that church inherited their praying DNA the same way the Onwuchekwa kids inherited their noses.

My parents and the pastors, preachers, and authors who have most influenced me were all mighty men and women of prayer. They put my best attempts at prayer to shame. I know what it looks like to be a prayer warrior (if you'll allow me to use that term) because I've witnessed it firsthand, not because I've exemplified it throughout my Christian life. For most of my journey, I've found myself deficient in the very qualities I admire.

MY TURNING POINT

A few years ago, something both terrible and wonderful happened. Six weeks before planting the church I currently pastor, my thirty-two-year-old brother suddenly died. No explanation. No cause of death. Nothing conclusive in the autopsy. No foul play. Just gone. Gone. For the first time in my life, I felt like all the wind was taken out of me. I couldn't breathe. If you've ever had the wind knocked out of you, then you know just how much it complicates everything. But this tragedy, in God's grace, was the best thing that could have ever happened for my relationship with the Lord and our church. God used a terrible situation to birth a wonderful thing in me.

I'm crying right now for the first time in months. I thought I had worked through my brother's death, but my heart is still incredibly tender as I reflect on this. Having the wind knocked out of me, literally and figuratively, was the tool God used to help me understand that prayer *is* breathing.

My filter vanished as my tongue was unhinged in prayer. I was both shocked and relieved, ashamed and angry at the words coming out of my mouth. I called God a liar. He seemed cruel and uncaring. Then in the same breath, I asked him to shower me with grace. I felt disdain, anger, hatred. And I told him. I couldn't help but tell him. It all just kept coming out. Pain felt like a truth serum that forced me to confess all of my unworthy thoughts of him. And he took it. Every ounce of it.

He corrected my negative view, not with words of rebuke but words of consolation.

While I was drowning in sorrow, he emptied my oxygen tank to force me to come up for air. When I came up to him, I wasn't met with the cold shoulder I deserved, but with open arms. Whatever I was doing before wasn't praying. It was formal, cold, sterile, rehearsed, and rote. For the first time in my life, I felt like I knew what it was to pray, to commune with God. When I offered the cares of my heart—every one of them— I met a God who wasn't as scared to take those cares on as I was to share them.

God transformed my brother's final breaths into some of my first. As a result, my whole life pivoted. And this forced a pivot in the church I was preparing to lead. By God's grace, this tragedy and several other hardships our church experienced early on helped to reinforce this often forgotten truth: prayer is vital and necessary to spiritual life. Prayer *is* like breathing.

THE KEY TO EFFECTIVE MINISTRY

I have pastored two churches over the past decade, and I've been involved with networks, organizations, seminaries, collectives, and other groups of Christians. I've sat with visionary leaders who have churches filled with great systems. I've also sat with leaders who aren't visionary and who have churches with poor systems. I've done ministry with gifted individuals, people with average gifts, and people with very little gifting or proficiency at all. I've partnered with attractional churches, missional churches, megachurches, medium churches, and meager churches. Throughout my experience, I've learned that these distinctions aren't the most important; they're peripheral and secondary. If I had to draw a line to create two categories of churches, it wouldn't follow these distinctions. I've learned to see churches as those that pray and those that don't. As I'll explain later, a church's commitment to prayer is one of the greatest determiners of its effectiveness in ministry.

Prayer is oxygen for the Christian. It sustains us. So it follows that prayer must be a source of life for any community of Christians. It is to the church what it is to individuals—breathing. Yet many of our gatherings could be likened to people coming together merely to hold their collective breath. This would explain why people seem to have so little energy for actually living out the Christian life.

But breathing together is what our churches need. Prayer humbles us like nothing else. When we pray, we're reminded that prayer is not like other disciplines in the world that require impressive aptitude and increased exercise to bring about great results. If someone hopes to get rewarded or compensated for playing an instrument, for example, then he must first achieve a level of expertise through years of practice. Great results spring from a grueling, long-term regimen. There's no initial payoff for novices of any kind.

Prayer isn't like that because great results don't come as a direct result of a grueling regimen and expertise. Great results come from our gracious Ruler, the great Rewarder and Reward of his people who cry out to him.

Many great accomplishments in prayer come from apparent novices. Abraham met God, and God offered to hear his prayer to spare the town where his nephew resided (Gen. 18:22–33). Moses met God at a burning bush, and not long after he successfully interceded for Israel (Ex. 32:31–34). In the forty days following Jesus's resurrection and ascension, the disciples began to pray differently. They stopped praying for self-preservation and more for gospel faithfulness and bold-ness (cf. Mark 8:31–34; Acts 4:23–31; 5:40–41). God rewards the prayers of novices, which encourages consistent prayer in the lives of his people.

If prayer is like breathing, then it isn't about our expertise. It's about our experiencing the power of the One to whom we pray. It's about the great expectations that grow in us when we have a genuine experience of the God who hears and answers. We don't need experts, and that's a strong encouragement to churches filled with many members and even pastors who feel like novices. I've experienced the beauty of weak prayers that meet a willing Savior. Our church has, too. It's a lot like taking the first breath after having the wind knocked out of you. The experience makes you eager to take another, and an-other, and another.

ABOUT THIS BOOK

This book won't talk much about prayer in the life of the indi-vidual Christian. There are better, more comprehensive works for that. This book is about prayer in the life of the church, and when it comes to corporate prayer, what do our churches need more than encouragement?

As someone who has helped lead churches of various sizes, budgets, and neighborhoods, I've had a wide range of relationships with other Christians and pastors. From my diverse experience, I've become convinced that prayer is among the most vital keys to a successful ministry. It's as necessary as breathing. It's not meant to replace work but enable it. If we want to see our churches thrive in faithfulness to God, then our churches must pray like their lives depended on it. We must learn how to breathe together.

My prayer is that this book doesn't have a long shelf life. There are wonderful Christian classics that will never lose their relevance until Christ returns. But my prayer is that soon, and very soon, a book like this would find as little of a market as I expect a book entitled *How to Breathe with Your Family at Dinner* would find.

My prayer is that this book will one day be more for edification when our energy wanes, and less for persuasion that our energies should be directed toward corporate prayer in the first place. My prayer is that regularly, fervently, and corporately crying out to our Father would be so ordinary and expected that it would be laughable that someone actually took time to write a book about it. I hope that happens one day. But since that day is not today, let's start this journey together and pray that God blesses it.

2

A CLASS ACT

Teach Us to Pray

NECESSARY ≠ NATURAL

In 2017, my wife and I received a phone call that would change our lives. For ten years we had tried to have a baby. For five years we tried to adopt. The phone call came on a Saturday, and by Monday we'd adopted our daughter.

The good news was that we finally had what we'd been praying for. The bad news was that she was born about two months premature and couldn't breathe on her own. We couldn't bring our baby girl home. She had to stay in the hospital for a few weeks, hooked up to a machine in order to learn how to breathe.

Breathing, the very thing necessary to her life being sustained, didn't come naturally to her. So it is with us and prayer. "To be a Christian without prayer is no more possible than to be alive without breathing" is still true. But just because something is necessary for life doesn't mean it comes naturally to us. It was true for my daughter's breathing, and it's true for our spiritual breathing as well.

Think back through the Bible at instances of people who needed prayer, and just how easy it was for them to avoid it.

How about Adam and Eve? After disobeying God and being spared from instant death, our gracious God came and initiated a conversation with them. At this point, they could have admitted their weakness and asked God for his help. They did neither. Instead, they attempted to redirect God's judgment to someone a little more "deserving."

Cain had a face-to-face conversation with God after being caught red-handed, but he neither admitted his weakness nor appealed for mercy. In Psalm 32, David admits that it was as natural as it was destructive to keep silent about his sin rather than pray. The disciples in Mark 14 realize that when lying prostrate, it's much easier to sleep than to offer supplication to God. Everyone who needs prayer the most finds out that it's unnatural.

TEACH US TO PRAY

One of the most ironic sequences of dialogue in Scripture is when the disciples ask Jesus how to pray (Luke 11:1). What makes it ironic isn't the fact that they're asking Jesus to teach them something. Jesus was God. He was wise, and they constantly referred to him as Rabbi and Teacher. This request stands out because this is the only record in Scripture when the disciples ask Jesus to teach them.

When it comes to Jesus's mighty acts and miracles, the disciples marvel at how he could calm the winds and waves. They stand in awe as Jesus heals the blind, casts out demons, and makes the lame walk. Peter doesn't ask how Jesus walks on water. He makes a request, and proceeds to walk out.

When Jesus sends out the seventy-two in Luke 10, he doesn't give step-by-step instructions on how to treat leprosy or cast out demons. He gives imperatives: heal the sick and proclaim the kingdom. None of the disciples say, "But Jesus, I was asleep the day you went over how much spittle to use when healing a blind man, or what to do when you find someone born blind versus someone who has gone blind." They take Jesus's mandate in stride and go with it, and they come back rejoicing that it actually worked.

Even when faced with their inability, like when they fail to cast out the demon in Mark 9, the disciples don't say to Jesus, "Teach us how to do that." Instead, they say, "Why couldn't we?" They seek a diagnosis as to what they did wrong, not a prescription for how to do it correctly.

But when it comes to prayer, the disciples say to Jesus, "Teach us" (Luke 11:1). They effectively say, "We need to learn. We know how to talk to our friends. We even know how to talk to you when you're right here. But prayer seems like something different, and it's something we don't know how to do."

Jesus responds with instructions, which synthesize how the Bible talks about prayer (see Matt. 6:9–13; Luke 11:2–4). Jesus has a way of putting handlebars on things. He takes the 613 commandments of the Old Testament, and sums them up in a few simple words: love God and love others. He does the same with the Bible's teaching on prayer. In a few stanzas, he provides a foundation for all our prayers.

LAYING A FOUNDATION: WHAT IS PRAYER?

We'll turn to those stanzas in the next two chapters. For now, we simply ask, What is prayer? It's been said that "definitions must always be the starting point for . . . two people entering into meaningful discussion."[1] We know that prayer is necessary; we know it doesn't come naturally to us. Like the disciples, we need to be taught how to pray. But it does us no good to talk about prayer and how it shapes the church if we can't first agree on what prayer is.

You may be saying, "This seems like a waste of time. Everybody knows what prayer is. You don't even have to be Christian to know what prayer is." Not so fast. Sometimes the most common words are the hardest to define.

How often have you used the word *so*? No one ever stops you midsentence to ask you to clarify your use of *so*. It seems like a word that doesn't need to be defined. But go ahead, define it (without a dictionary or Google).

You see what I mean? It's a word that's easier to use than to define. Sometimes, the most common words cause the most confusion, and *prayer* isn't exempt.

Definitions for prayer abound. Here are a few:

Prayer is talking to God. Just talk to God like you would talk to your best friend. You don't need to learn to talk to God. Just do it.

Prayer is demanding something from God. Prayer is our decreeing and demanding that God would do what we want him to do. It's wrestling with him until he gives us what we want. God plays hard to get in order to see just how much we want what we pray for. We have to demand what we want from him. We need to name it and claim it.

Prayer is aligning our will with God's. Prayer isn't about getting anything from God or causing him to act. He knows what you need and has already determined if he's going to give it to you. Prayer is really all about aligning your will to his. Prayer is more for you than it is for God.

Prayer is wishful thinking aimed in God's direction. Prayer is nothing more than well wishes when you hear about a tragedy, or wishful thinking when you hear someone is hopeful about an outcome.

Prayer is some combination of all of these things.

Who's right? We can't just settle for any definition. We need the right one. Why? Because misinterpretation leads to misapplication.

Did you ever hear the story about the guy who got his mom an expensive parrot for Mother's Day? He paid $10,000 for a parrot that could speak forty languages and sing a few hymns. He sent the bird to his mom and didn't hear back for a few days. Nervous that she didn't like the bird, he called his mom and asked her, "How'd you like the bird?" to which she replied, "It was great!" Filled with pride, the son asked, "What was your favorite part?" She answered, "The thighs. They were delicious." Wrong interpretation, wrong application.

WHAT PRAYER IS NOT

Time won't allow us to address each of the definitions, but let's talk briefly about a few common ways people think about prayer.

Exodus 33:11 tells us that Moses talked with God face-to-face as a man talks to a friend. I think it's possible to build a faulty theology of prayer based on a misapplication of this verse. While part of prayer is talking to God as you would a friend, this definition by itself is an oversimplification.

Jesus was God in the flesh. So every time the disciples had a conversation with Jesus, they were talking to God just as they would talk to anyone else. If prayer meant merely talking to God, and Jesus was God, then shouldn't we see every conversation someone had with Jesus as prayer? I don't think Jesus saw it that way.

When Philip asks Jesus to show them the Father, Jesus replies, "Whoever has seen me has seen the Father" (John 14:9). Jesus seems to say, "Look no further. If you've seen me, you've seen God" (see Heb. 1:3). When the disciples ask Jesus to teach them how to pray, however, he doesn't respond in the same way. He doesn't say, "Well, if you've talked to me, you've talked to the Father." Instead, he gives them instructions. He gives them a template on how to address someone other than the person standing right in front of them: "Our Father" (Matt. 6:9–15; see also Luke 11:1–4).

While prayer is more than casual conversation with our Creator, it's far from twisting God's arm to get what we want. God is all-powerful. We can't twist his arm. He's too strong. We can't barter with him any more than my infant daughter can barter with me—she doesn't own anything I need or want. We can't demand anything from God because it's impossible for someone without needs to be coerced.

See what I mean by the difficulty of understanding what prayer is? It's not as cut-and-dried as the definitions we may have grown up with and taken for granted.

CALLING ON THE NAME OF THE LORD

I'm forever indebted to Gary Millar's book on prayer, *Calling on the Name of the Lord: A Biblical Theology of Prayer*. His book is simply an answer to the question: What exactly is prayer? He looks for the common thread that weaves every instance of prayer from Genesis to Revelation to create a biblical definition of prayer that's specific yet comprehensive. Here's what he concludes: prayer is "calling on God to come through on his promise."[2]

The first instance of recorded prayer in the Bible occurs in Genesis 4, outside of the garden of Eden: "And Adam knew his wife again, and she bore a son and called his name Seth, for she said, 'God has appointed for me another offspring instead of Abel, for Cain killed him.' To Seth also a son was born, and he called his name Enosh. At that time people began to call upon the name of the LORD" (Gen. 4:25–26).

Calling on the name of the Lord is more than just saying his name aloud. Throughout the Bible, the name of the Lord is synonymous with the nature of the Lord. To call on his name is to make an appeal to his character. It's a cry for help, like when someone shouts, "Call 911!" We don't ask, "After I call 911, what do you think the nature of the conversation should be?" To call 911 is to make an appeal for help based on what we know 911 *is*—an emergency line. The same is true for calling on the name of the Lord.

Genesis 4:26 is what Millar calls a "load-bearing" verse.[3] Non-load-bearing walls can be knocked down without compromising the structural integrity of a house. Load-bearing walls, on the other hand, can't be knocked down without the house collapsing. Verse 26 carries this kind of heavy load when it comes to understanding what it means to pray. It helps us to build a framework for how we should understand prayer, since it's the first time in the Bible we see people calling on the name of the Lord.

Here's the backdrop of that load-bearing verse. In Genesis 1 and 2, God creates a perfect world, and he places Adam and Eve in it to relate to him and reflect his glory throughout all creation. In Genesis 3, Adam and Eve are fooled by the serpent, and they decide to replace God rather than reflect him. When God confronts them about their sin, Adam blames Eve, and Eve blames the serpent.

Then God begins to speak. What does he say? In Genesis 3:15 (another load-bearing verse) he speaks a word of promise. One day, the seed of the woman will crush the snake. The woman will have a child who will defeat this deceiver. Although Adam and Eve sinned, God graciously preserves their lives and promises he will one day make things right through this Son.

So Genesis 4 is hopeful at the beginning. Adam and Eve have a son, and they believe their firstborn is God's promise fulfilled. They give him the name Cain, which means "acquired." They assume he is the covenant seed testified about in Genesis 3:15. But after Cain comes back from the first church picnic with his brother's blood on his hands, he's banished by God, and it becomes apparent to everyone that he isn't the promised seed God was talking about.

The rest of Genesis 4 is a genealogy of Cain's descendants that ends with a distant relative named Lamech. Murder runs through the family of Cain, and Lamech now brags about how he has outdone his great-great-great-granddad. That's where verses 25 and 26 come in.

Adam and Eve have another son, Seth, who offers a contrast. These people want God to fulfill his promise, even if that day isn't today. When people begin to call on the name of the Lord, they are "calling on God to come through on his promise" of a son who will reverse the curse and defeat the serpent.[4]

John Calvin asserts, "Prayer in the Bible is intimately linked with the gospel—God's promised and provided solution to the problem of human rebellion against him and its consequences. The gospel shape of prayer is evident from the opening pages of the Bible—and in particular in Genesis 4:26, when people first begin to 'call on the name of Yahweh'—right through the end, when the church prays, 'Come, Lord Jesus!' (see Rev. 22:20)."[5] In a sense, then, prayer is saying, "Are we there yet, God? Please bring about the things that you promised you would." Prayer in the Bible is linked to the hope of redemption and, thus, the gospel.

PRAYER: GOD'S PRESCRIPTION FOR LIFE IN A FALLEN WORLD

Think of prayer as God's prescription for life in a fallen world. This prescription works like any other. Imagine being prescribed a medication for an ailment that's been bothering you. You may leave the doctor's office with nothing but a sheet of paper, but something changes. What causes you to smile even when your present sickness is severe and your circumstances haven't changed? One word: *hope*. A prescription isn't the medication itself. It merely connects you to the medicine. Your illness may still be bothering you, but the prescription reminds you that your sickness is temporary because you've found a solution.

Like a prescription, prayer eases our concerns before repairing our circumstances. Take Psalm 13. We're unsure of the exact circumstance that led David to pen this psalm, but everyone who reads it has had similar experiences.

Psalm 13 begins with David's depression: "How long, O LORD? Will you forget me forever? How long will you hide your face from me?" (v. 1). But by the end, David is celebrating deliverance: "I will sing to the LORD, because he has dealt bountifully with me" (v. 6). The psalm is only six verses long. How did David go from depression to deliverance that quickly? Not by his circumstances changing, but by taking his concerns to God, asking him to do what he said he would do, and being confident that he would do it.

David learns that prayer is more about "Will you? Won't you?" than it is about "When will you?" Though he starts out concerned with the timing of God, he resolves by the end of the psalm to rejoice in the God who loves him and will deliver him. God's character and promises preserved David's joy, even when his circumstance hadn't yet changed. Like a prescription, prayer provided the hope that David needed to persevere: God has made a promise, and he always makes good on his promises.

JESUS'S ENCOURAGEMENT

There's nothing more humbling than asking someone to teach you how to do something. Thankfully, Jesus doesn't spend time beating his followers up; instead, he builds them up, highlighting the many incentives of prayer. Through his parables and other stories, Jesus highlights what we're missing out on when we don't pray.

When teaching about prayer, Jesus graciously reminds us that God sees us—not in the way a camera sees someone committing a crime, but in the way an undercover boss rewards an employee who is doing something right. Match that truth with Jesus's reminder that prayers are measured by their strength and not their length, and all of our insecurities should vanish. Our Lord's instructions leave us with no excuse for not praying, and every encouragement to pray in light of our hope.

THE CHURCH SHAPE OF PRAYER

This hope is shared among all Christians. It's the hope that governs our lives (see 1 Tim. 4:10; Titus 1:1–2; 2:11–14; 3:4–7). This means that hope for the Christian is *ours*, not just mine. As Mark Dever says, "It's impossible to answer the question *what is a Christian?* without ending up in a conversation about the church—at least, in the Bible it is."[6] If prayer clings to the hope we share in Christ, then prayer should reflect our togetherness in Christ. If prayer has a gospel shape, then by implication it must have a church shape.

In this book we won't look at every instance of prayer in the Bible. We'll spend the majority of our time on two. That's not to say that the others aren't important. It's merely to help us understand what prayer should look like as a pattern and in practice. And what better model of prayer do we have than the one our Lord Jesus provides? His instruction and example will help us build a framework that will allow us to better understand prayer and its corporate implications.

3

THE WORLD IS YOURS

A Family Led

Here's our problem: prayerlessness is spiritual suicide. So what I'm suggesting is that we pray more. Not rocket science, I know. But before we can pray more, we must know what we mean by *prayer*. How do we learn a biblical definition of prayer? Jesus graciously teaches us.

These next two chapters will work through the two parts of Jesus's template for Christian prayer. This will lay the groundwork for us to understand the necessity of corporate prayer and how it shapes the church.

PRIORITIES OVER PROCESS: BEGINNING TO LEARN HOW TO PRAY

My two-year-old nephew Jackson didn't know cake existed until his first Thanksgiving, when our neighbors brought over a pound cake. His entire life changed. A palette formerly accustomed to Similac, pureed fruits and vegetables, crayons, dirt, and combinations of all of the above was now exposed to a combination of flavors that did something different for him. Shortly after deducing that the name of this new pleasure was *cake*, he realized he could have it on demand from his gullible uncle if he simply uttered the word in commanding fashion: "Cake! Cake!" Every time he'd come over, the first word out of his mouth would be "Cake!" I, of course, was a sucker and would give it to him . . . until my wife intervened.

"Jackson, if you want cake, that's not how we ask. If you want cake, you say, 'Cake please.'" From that point on, we began to catechize little Jackson. Whenever he would demand "Cake!" we'd respond, "Jackson, how do you ask for cake?" to which he'd promptly respond, "Cake pwease!" We taught Jackson the right process to get what he wanted. We didn't call into question the thing he desired.

Jesus approaches prayer differently. He doesn't correct our process problem, like my wife and I did. He addresses our priorities problem. J. C. Ryle asserts, "Tell me what a man's prayers are, and I will soon tell you the state of his soul."[1] As Jesus teaches us to pray, he doesn't begin by teaching us how to ask. Instead, he teaches us what to ask for. He gives us our priorities before he gives us a process. So that's where we'll begin.

OUR FATHER: PRAYER BEGINS WITH EMBRACING RELATIONSHIPS

The first two words of the Lord's Prayer—"Our Father"—are as important as they are familiar (Matt. 6:9). But don't let their familiarity blind you to their significance. Prayer begins with embracing not just a relationship, but *relationships*. We're used to thinking of prayer as personally and individually relating to God, but it's more than that.

While practicing prayer in isolation may seem like a good

safeguard against the temptation to impress others with our prayers (Matt. 6:5), praying always and only by ourselves may be an overcorrection. From feeding the five thousand (John 6:10–11) to raising Lazarus from the dead (John 11:41–44) to entering the garden of Gethsemane (Matt. 26:36), Jesus often involved others in his prayers. We certainly shouldn't try to impress others with our prayers, but we should always involve them in our prayers.

Why? Because we're family. God is not just my Father, but "Our Father." These two words remind us that we're both children of God and siblings to each other. Prayer was never meant to be a merely personal exercise with personal benefits, but a discipline that reminds us how we're personally responsible for others. This means that every time we pray, we should actively reject an individualistic mindset. We're not just individuals in relationship with God, but we are part of a community of people who have the same access to God. Prayer is a collective exercise.

In case you think I'm reading too much into this, notice that throughout the Sermon on the Mount (Matthew 5–7), Jesus tends to use singular pronouns when speaking to the crowd about morality. His instructions on lust (5:29–30), adultery and divorce (5:32–33), and vengeance (5:39–42) are all in the singular. But when talking to this same crowd about prayer, all of his pronouns are plural (6:9–13). This isn't a grammatical slip. This is Jesus instructing us.

We're family because we have the same Father. Before we request anything in prayer, we're reminded that God is not merely our sovereign Judge and Ruler. He's also our Father. Jesus died as the substitute for our sin to justify us (declare us righteous) in God's courtroom. But he justified us so that he might adopt us into his family.[2] This means that when we come to God, we have nothing to fear.

Do you see how astonishing this is? Our Father listens and inclines his ear to us (Ps. 5:1–3). Our Father shows us compassion despite our flaws and weaknesses (Ps. 103:13). Our Father covers us with his love, even though we deserve his wrath (Rom. 8:1, 15). Our Father takes care of our needs and gives us good gifts (Matt. 6:8; 7:11; James 1:17). Our Father even disciplines us in love for our good (Heb. 12:5–11). What a privilege to call God our Father!

J. I. Packer says it best:

> If you want to judge how well a person understands Christianity, find out how much he makes of the thought of being God's child, and having God as his Father. If this is not the thought that prompts and controls his worship and prayers and his whole outlook on life, it means that he does not understand Christianity very well at all. For everything that Christ taught, everything that makes the New Testament new and better than the Old, everything that is distinctly Christian as opposed to merely Jewish, is summed up in the knowledge of the Fatherhood of God. "Father" is the Christian name for God.[3]

Throughout my life I've been blessed to witness many great fathers. My own is my hero. But over the past decade, I've seen two exceptional fathers who were fellow pastors with me. Both of them father sons with autism. What the world sees as an imperfection or a liability doesn't take away the abundance of love they have for their sons. I've watched them love their sons unconditionally, way past the point where many other men become frustrated with their children.

This is the blessing of the fatherhood of God to us. It's not for those who are perfect or elite by any stretch of the imagination. None of us is the star athlete, the successful entrepreneur, or the articulate artist whom other fathers are envious to have. Rather, we are the prodigal son, squandering our God-given dignity on things that don't satisfy. We are children desperately in need of a Father willing to constantly give unconditional love because we constantly fail at all the conditions. God alone can be this kind of Father to us.

The same God who prepares our hearts to pray inclines his ear to hear us. This is one of the great incentives to pray. You have someone who truly, fully listens. No amount of infirmity or blemish could make him avoid us. Our Father has his ear inclined to us, and he's eager to hear from us even now. I don't know how long it's been since you've prayed to him, but here's something I'm sure of: he's listening. And he's a better listener than we could ever imagine.

When we pray "Our Father," we remind ourselves of his closeness, his wisdom, his patience, and his care. Time doesn't allow us to discuss the limitless applications to this truth. But just know this: God calls us first and foremost to embrace our relationship with him as Father.

WHO IS IN HEAVEN: UNDERSTANDING HIS POWER

Our Father is "in heaven" (Matt. 6:9). We begin prayer with more than the warm fuzzies of embracing our relationships to our Father and each other; we begin with a settled confidence of asking someone who is at the top of the pecking order. When biblical authors speak of heaven, not only are they referring to a place or location but they are also referencing a statement of power. When we say that Barack Obama was in the White House, we mean more than his address. We mean that he held the highest office in the land. He had power. This is what the biblical authors mean by saying that our Father is in heaven.

Think of Psalm 115:3: "Our God is in the heavens; he does all that he pleases." Sure enough, when humanity "threatened" God's command by building a tower that would reach "heaven" (Genesis 11), God had to come down a few stairs to see the top of these so-called towers. He then flexed his power and confused their languages, dispersing the people over the face of the earth. When we pray, we are holding on to God's omnipotence. He is in control. He needs permission from no one. He is coerced by none. No one can stop his plans. Our Father in heaven is capable! His agenda always wins.

PUTTING IT TOGETHER: GOD IS AS COMPASSIONATE AS HE IS CAPABLE

"Our Father in heaven" sets the backdrop of our prayers (Matt. 6:9). These first four words invite us to pray because they teach us that God is as compassionate as he is capable. He can do anything. And because Jesus's sacrificial death makes Christians a part of his family, we know he listens and is inclined to respond favorably to what we ask. There's no court of appeals that can undo the decisions he makes. We have the ear of the most powerful being in and over the universe. He sees all, knows all, directs all.

So the question becomes this: If you had the ear and the favor of the most powerful being in the universe, what would you ask for? A larger tax return at the end of the year? A good report at your next doctor's visit? Knowing that the most powerful being in the world is inclined to respond favorably to me excites me, as I'm sure it does you. I don't know you, but I'm sure your requests wouldn't be exactly the same as mine. We're complex creatures with complex concerns and problems. But there's likely something weighing on your heart right now. What you request from God this week may affect next week.

How should the knowledge of God's power and compassion impact our praying? First, it should make us bold. A. W. Tozer puts it this way: "Prayer unites God and the praying man in one and says, God is omnipotent and the praying man is omnipotent (for the time being), because he is in touch with omnipotence."[4] Do you understand that this type of power is at your disposal in prayer? This is what Jesus wants us to know.

Second, it should make us humble. The author of Ecclesiastes instructs, "Be not rash with your mouth, nor let your heart be hasty to utter a word before God, for God is in heaven and you are on earth. Therefore let your words be few" (5:2). God is not here to simply grant wishes. He's not here to fund idolatry. God does serve us, but he exists for his glory. We exist for him, not the other way around. In prayer, we embrace the right posture of longing for his glory before his provision.

GOD'S PRESENCE > GOD'S PROVISION

In the Lord's Prayer (Matt. 6:9–13), Jesus helps us understand where our requests should begin. After establishing that God is our Father who is as compassionate as he is capable, Jesus reminds us that God's power aims to advance his agenda, not ours. Jesus shows us that Christian prayer begins with longing for God's presence before his provision.

All of the requests at the beginning of the Lord's Prayer are godward. Take a look:

> Our Father in heaven,
> hallowed be *your* name.
> *Your* kingdom come.
> *Your* will be done
>   on earth as it is in heaven. (Matt. 6:9–10)

This removes man from the center of the picture. It displaces our needs and desires, reminding us that the most important things about prayer are not what God gives us by way of his possessions, but what God gives by way of his presence. Throughout the Bible, the people who gain peace and security in this life are the people who long for God's presence more than his possessions. Jesus teaches us this in his first three petitions.

First Petition: God's Honor

"Hallowed be your name" (Matt. 6:9) could better be translated for our ears, "I pray that your name will be honored." In the Old Testament, when people lived against God's will and design, their wicked deeds were said to profane the name of God. To pray "hallowed be your name" means being concerned more with the advancement of God's reputation in the world than your own. It's praying that God himself would protect his name from being defamed and obscured, so that people don't accept a wrong picture of him or reject a distorted picture of him. God's name is holy. Nothing can change that reality. We're simply asking him to work in the world so that his name would be treated as such.

The glory of God has come into the world in the person of Jesus. "Hallowed be your name" therefore means praying that everyone would respond appropriately to Jesus. The world we live in is as unimpressed with God as someone who stays seated when the bride walks down the aisle. This is because they're blinded to the glory of God as revealed in Jesus (see 2 Cor. 4:3–6). So we begin prayer by pleading that God's glory would be seen and submitted to in the person of Christ. The beauty of this petition is that we're asking God to do what he already wants to do.

This request sets the tone for the rest of the prayer. All that we ask of God must flow from this all-consuming desire.

Second Petition: God's Kingdom Come

"Your kingdom come" (Matt. 6:10) is a prayer for the success of the gospel in the world. We know the gospel has changed us, so we plead for God's kingdom to be extended through the gospel going out to the ends of the world.

We're tired of the world we live in, and we long for something better. We want to experience the fullness of the Beatitudes. We long to be where God's rule is recognized and adored. God has promised this will happen, and his promise stokes our longing. When a dad promises his daughter that he will take her to Disneyland, the child knows this trip isn't a matter of if, but when. In her eagerness to receive the fulfillment of her dad's promise, she constantly asks, "When are we going? You promised!" This is what it's like for us to pray "your kingdom come."

We cannot serve two masters. Likewise, two kings—us and God—cannot coexist. Someone's rule and ambitions have to die. As Christians, our agendas have in fact died, and it's glorious because ours would have killed us (Gal. 2:20). Praying "your will be done, on earth as it is in heaven" unifies us because it helps us long for his kingdom. It keeps us from backbiting, from jockeying for position, from longing to establish little kingdoms of our own.

Third Petition: Your Will Be Done

"Your will be done, on earth as it is in heaven" (Matt. 6:10) further develops the second request for God's kingdom to come. We long to see God reign here on earth in the same way he already reigns in heaven. We don't want people to submit reluctantly to God's rule. We want them to joyfully submit because they're convinced he is good. We pray for God's will to be accomplished on earth however he determines, even if it means our suffering, sacrifice, and death.

Establishing God's kingdom on earth means displacing lesser kingdoms, which is what churches do through their gospel work. Local churches, after all, are outposts of God's kingdom. So praying that his will would be done means praying that God would continue to establish his gospel work through local churches.

This prayer for God's presence to be seen and enjoyed is quite startling to a world that prefers for God to be an absentee

Father that just sends a big child support check each month. Because we're sinful, we would prefer God to give us our demands while demanding nothing in return. We love to set the agenda. But Jesus teaches us here that God's presence precedes his provision. His agenda is far better than ours.

When our local churches pray and live in light of these first three petitions, it's attractive to the watching world because we display a different picture about what God is like. It shows the world how ineffective its kingdoms are. It strengthens our witness.

THE REAL PROBLEM: APATHY, NOT ABSENCE

As we begin to pray this way, we're reminded of a few things. First, the world exists as a canvas for God's glory. Second, what we need most is for God to fix what's wrong. The true problem isn't God's absence from the world. He's omnipresent. The real problem is our apathy to God's presence, which manifests itself through self-centeredness and self-concern. This in turn crowds out our ability to love and honor others—especially the God who created us.

How often do you find yourself unable to eat, sleep, or focus because you're so frustrated with how God's name is being disrespected? How often do you find yourself in anguish to the point of prayer over the fact that God's kingdom and purposes are disregarded? Does that make it into your prayer journal? Do you see the absence of God's honor as the main problem with the world? With your marriage? With your church? Jesus is teaching us to cry out to God for these things, not because he needs help doing it, but because we need help desiring it. Our agenda conflicts with God's agenda because our affections conflict with his. And our affections are what ultimately shape our agenda, especially in prayer.

It's easy and natural to pray about our honor, our kingdoms, and our purposes. How do you respond when you're disrespected, dishonored, and disregarded? Your affections are often revealed most clearly when you're angry. It's natural for us to pray, "God, help them to treat me with the respect and dignity I deserve." How easy it is to cry out to God when we feel like circumstances are threatening our kingdoms and personal projects. When do you find yourself most angry and upset with God? If you're anything like me, it's when you feel he has done something that crosses your will. We essentially pray, "God, please let everything work out the way I want it to. Help me build my own kingdom."

Good prayers and bad prayers aren't distinguished based on their morality. God doesn't just say no to prayers for help in robbing a bank. It's possible to pray for things that are good and acceptable, while still effectively asking God to fund our idolatry. Our self-centeredness is like gravity; it pulls us down. Jesus is teaching us to aim higher. He wants our prayers to soar.

GOD IS NOT A GENIE

By praying for God's priorities to settle in our hearts, we reject the false notion that God is a genie. I'm no genie expert, but movies and TV shows with genies show us something interesting: no one struggles to talk to his genie the way Christians struggle to talk to God in prayer. They don't forget to ask for things. They don't treat conversation with their genies as a last resort. No one has a problem talking with his or her genie because a genie always grants the asker's request. The genie has one job: to advance the agenda of the one to whom he's bound.

But when we pray as Jesus taught, we're reminded that God's presence and person is precious—far more precious than his provision. God sets the agenda, and this is best for us. So, as we pray this way together, he forms us into a community of people who confess that our dependency on him is *not* primarily circumstantial. We need God *always*, and our joy comes from Jesus's presence first and foremost, regardless of what we get in terms of material provision. And you know what? As this truth is cemented in our hearts through prayer, God in his kindness grants us a greater experience of his presence.

The Lord's Prayer is supernatural. Sure, anyone can parrot the words, but only those who have been internally changed truly desire what it asks for. The words are not a magical incantation. Saying them out loud isn't the goal. Slave owners probably recited the Declaration of Independence's "All men are created equal" hundreds of times. Parroting words does no good. Jesus isn't creating parrots, but pray-ers.

If you truly know what it means to call God your Father, you want his glory to spread to every corner of the earth. No other request is big enough.

And remember, we're asking him to do what he already wants to do.

A FAMILY UNIFIED

It's easy for churches to fall into competing agendas and conflicting affections (see James 4:1–4). A community of sinful, not-fully-sanctified people living in close proximity will step on each other's toes. A diverse Christian community has a diversity of affections, which can lead to a diversity of visions.

Yet these conflicts fall by the wayside when we pray as Jesus taught.

If your life's primary concern is to make your name great, you'll be uncomfortable in Christian community. After all, being sinned against is inevitable. But if your primary concern is to make God's name great—to advance his honor, kingdom, and purpose in the world—then the presence of sin in your community, perhaps even your own, offers an opportunity to advance his agenda by a Christlike response.

Can God's name be glorified in the face of injustice? Absolutely. As Jesus unjustly died on the cross, a Roman centurion honored Jesus's name as holy (Mark 15:39). Jesus himself displayed God's mercy by praying, "Father, forgive them." So even our trials serve as a way for us to show the forgiveness of God and thus honor his name.

Jesus sets the priority and agenda for our prayers. As churches come together and pray in line with the Lord's Prayer, we're reminded of this shared desire: for the King of kings to come and rule. It helps us to stop jockeying for position, but instead to plead for God to take his rightful position in our church and the world. It recalibrates our compasses and synchronizes our watches, so that we're all headed in the same direction. It brings unity. It reminds us that no matter our circumstance—rich or poor, old or young, married or single, majority or minority—we all need the same thing: God's precious presence.

4

SOUL FOOD

A Family Fed

SOUL FOOD: HAVING A MEAL TOGETHER

One of my greatest frustrations in life is commercialized soul food. Having lived in Atlanta for almost a decade, I can speak on this with a level of expertise. Atlanta is full of places that attempt to offer people the food they want while taking away the inconvenience of a long wait. Theoretically, the food is the same. But when you remove the slow care in cooking and convert it into an individualized take-out meal, you change what soul food is. You cheapen it.

The wait is an essential part of soul food, because soul food is about family and friends. It's about coming together and enjoying each other while waiting. It's about resting together afterward, lethargic in our food comas.

We should think of prayer this way, too. I believe this is Jesus's intention as he preaches the second half of the Lord's Prayer.

PRAYING FOR PROVISION: MORE THAN NEEDS BEING MET

Prayer begins with longing for God's presence before his provision. But prayer shouldn't end there. We still need things from

God. Just because he tells us not to prioritize food and clothing doesn't mean we don't need food and clothing. Jesus invites us to ask for three things in particular: provision, pardon, and protection. These aren't the only things we can ask God for, but they provide a template for what we should prioritize.

Provision

Jesus first tells us to ask for "our daily bread" (Matt. 6:11). Notice, he wants us to pray for *daily* bread—not weekly bread, not monthly bread, not a trust fund, not a nice little nest egg. He wants us to rely upon God *daily*. Jesus's point here is similar to Agur's in Proverbs 30:8–9. Agur prays:

> Give me neither poverty nor riches;
>> feed me with the food that is needful for me,
> lest I be full and deny you
>> and say, "Who is the LORD?"
> or lest I be poor and steal
>> and profane the name of my God.

Do you see? Agur isn't simply interested in having his needs met. He wants to ensure the name of God isn't profaned—whether with too much or too little. Too much says God is unnecessary. Too little says he is unconcerned. "So give me just what I need today, and I'll come back tomorrow. Keep me constantly dependent on you so that every day the way I relate to your provision says you're the sufficient supplier of my needs." Jesus, likewise, doesn't mean for our *asking* to move beyond the *praising* we discussed in the last chapter ("hallowed be your name"). The way we relate to food and possessions either accentuates or diminishes the presentation of God's glory through us. The prayer for provision and the prayer of praise are inseparable, and the daily nature of our dependence makes this point.

We're accustomed to praying for our meals right before we eat. But we're not accustomed to getting out of bed every morning and asking God to feed us. Why? Because we, at least in the West, have bank accounts, jobs, gift cards, and people who owe us lunch. We're confident that we'll eat. We give little thought to starvation. The idea of praying this way in the morning seems like a formality. We take God's provision for granted because we think we earned it through our grit and diligence. At the same time, we begin to think we never have enough.

This type of pride fosters a lack of gratitude. And when gratitude leaves the room, greed quickly enters and sprawls out, leaving no room for anyone else. Greedy people essentially say, "I've worked hard for my things so I should enjoy them. Why should I have to take care of someone who's been irresponsible?" Thinking our provision comes by our own grit, we also think we should determine how it's distributed.

But Jesus won't allow that. He commands us to pray for our bread daily so that we're reminded that every last gift is from God.

Pardon

Jesus next tells us to pray, "And forgive us our debts, as we also have forgiven our debtors" (Matt. 6:12). This request lies at the heart of true Christianity. It reminds us that peace with

God always comes through pardon and forgiveness, never performance. Jesus's life, death, and resurrection on our behalf is our only appeal for forgiveness. We're not asking for God to reconsider our debt, nor are we asking for more time to pay our debt. We're asking for forgiveness. We don't earn it. We go to God for it. And as often as we pray for bread, we're to pray for forgiveness. In so doing, we're daily reminded of at least two things: (1) our consistent failings, and (2) God's eagerness to forgive. To miss a day of praying this way is to spend a day where I'm tempted to think that God and I are okay because of my performance. That's never been the case, nor will it ever be.

When our hearts aren't convinced of our need for God's forgiveness, we're prone to hold grudges. We'll focus on other people's debts (see Matt. 18:21–35). We're sure to withhold forgiveness.

Do you see how we daily and desperately need to pray, "And forgive us our debts, as we also have forgiven our debtors" (Matt. 6:12)? Jesus knows that in order for us to honor God's name, we need a fresh reminder of our sin and God's grace every day.

Protection

Finally, Jesus instructs us to pray, "And lead us not into temptation, but deliver us from evil" (Matt. 6:13). Like pardon from past sin, protection from future sin is found in Jesus. It must be given. The trouble is, we either respond to temptation with anxiety, thinking that we'll never change, or we respond with arrogance, assuming we have the power to resist.

Yet Jesus tells us to pray for provision, pardon, and

protection not just so we can get them, but so we're shaped by the requests we make. He commands us to pray for the things we're tempted to get ourselves because anything we can get ourselves, we eventually take for granted, which dishonors God's name.

PRAYING FOR OUR FAMILY WITH PLURAL PRONOUNS

When Jesus taught the disciples how to pray, he wanted them to remember the needs of others, not just their own needs. So he continues to use plural pronouns: "Give us . . . forgive us . . . lead us . . ." Certainly this applies to praying in public spaces. When praying in a group, involve others by praying with words like "we" and "us."

Yet even when we pray alone, we should have our neighbors in mind. We should be consumed with ways to love them. If we really believe Jesus is good enough to give something to us, we must believe he's good enough to give it to others. Praying with plural pronouns as Jesus taught is one of the best ways to love our neighbors because, even when they're out of sight, they should never be out of mind.

When you are praying for good things like provision, pardon, and protection, who comes to mind when you think of "us"? I imagine it's people you're fond of, people you like.

But do you also ask God for the provision, pardon, and protection of people who frustrate you and get on your nerves? How often do you pray for them? Do you bump people off the prayer list until they get their act together? It's tough to include our enemies in the "us" category. We may not pray for their destruction or downfall, but we don't really pray much for their flourishing either, do we? Our prayers are for help in dealing with them, but that's not the same thing as praying for their well-being.

It's possible that when praying with first-person plural pronouns (*us* and *we*), no one specific comes to mind, just a group of silhouettes. But vague prayers for silhouettes don't help our brothers and sisters. If anything, they're a sign of neglect. People aren't helped, and God isn't honored. J. C. Ryle states:

> It should not be enough to confess we are sinners; we should name the sins of which our conscience tells us we are most guilty. It should not be enough to ask for holiness; we should name the graces in which we feel most deficient. It should not be enough to tell the Lord we are in trouble; we should describe our trouble and all its peculiarities. . . . What should we think of the patient who told his doctor he was ill, but never went into particulars? What should we think of the wife who told her husband she was unhappy, but did not specify the cause? What should we think of the child who told his father he was in trouble, but nothing more? Christ is the true bridegroom of the soul, the true physician of the heart, the real father of all his people. Let us show that we feel this by being unreserved in our communications with him.[1]

Ryle's wisdom doesn't just apply to us individually, but corporately. We run out of things to pray about when we pray vague prayers for vague people. It's easy to cover our bases and leave God's presence just as unimpressed and underwhelmed as when we came. But if our prayers begin to be filled with particular requests for particular people, we remove the dangers associated with silhouettes. We begin to see the delight that comes from praying specific needs for specific people.

Ryle continues:

> We are all selfish by nature, and our selfishness is very apt to stick to us, even when we are converted. There is a tendency in us to think only of our own souls, our own spiritual conflicts, our own progress in religion, and to forget others. Against this tendency we all have need to watch and strive, and not least in our prayers. We should study to be of a public spirit. We should stir ourselves up to name other names besides our own before the throne of grace. We should try to bear in our hearts the whole world, the heathen, the Jews, the Roman Catholics, the body of true believers, the professing Protestant churches, the country in which we live, the congregation to which we belong, the household in which we sojourn, the friends and relations we are connected with. For each and all of these we should plead. This is the highest charity. He loves me best who loves me in his prayers. This is for our soul's health. It enlarges our sympathies and expands our hearts. This is for the benefit of the church. The wheels of all machinery for extending the gospel are moved by prayer. They do as much for the Lord's cause who intercede like Moses on the mount, as they do who fight like Joshua in the thick of the battle. This is to be like Christ. He bears the names of his people, as their High Priest, before the Father. Oh, the privilege of being like Jesus! This is to be a true helper to ministers. If I must choose a congregation, give me a people that pray.[2]

Ryle wasn't content to leave the "us" undefined, and we shouldn't be either. The local church is a glove that fits snugly around corporate prayer. Of course, there are ways to pray corporately and obey the spirit of this command without the local church. But I believe the local church is the best way to define the "us" in our prayers. The local church serves as a greenhouse where our prayers thrive. The local church creates the ideal environment for us to maximize the benefits of prayer while mitigating the dangers of selfishness and pride described above.

All Christians should have the benefit of being a member of a local church. The local church offers its own kind of fulfillment of Genesis 2:18: "It is not good that the man should be alone." The Christian may be an orphan in the world with no earthly family. He may not have a spouse, or he may lose the spouse he loved. The Christian may be ostracized by the culture for his beliefs. He may find himself surrounded by people of a completely different cultural background. But the Christian in covenant with a local church is never alone. As long as the church endures, which will be for all eternity, the Christian is always part of an "us." The local church takes the theory of Christianity and makes it tangible—in love, deed, and especially in prayer.

Consider how the "us" of corporate prayer works with regard to provision. Let's say I pray for God to provide for "our" needs, and I end up getting a raise while someone else loses his job. I can't just say, "I'm praying for you to be warm and fed" (see James 2:15–16). No, I must work out my faith in prayer by presuming that God providentially answered our prayers for provision by giving me more than I need and giving someone else less than what he needs. In this way God, through my prayer, is removing greed from me by providing an opportunity to freely give the gift he's given to me. Simultaneously, God is removing pride from my brother by putting him in a position where he gets to accept God's good gifts from another brother. Far from being a charity case, he becomes a canvas displaying God's wisdom and goodness in response to our asking for provision.

How does the "us" work in our prayers for pardon and protection? Let's say I pray that God would forgive me of my sin. Then, in the midst of praying for specific people in my church, a silhouette is filled in with a specific person who has offended me. I don't feel ready to forgive that person. What then? Now I have a decision to make. I can plead with God to forgive me of my hypocrisy and help me in the area of forgiveness, and I can enjoy a restored relationship with my brother. Or, I can pretend like the hypocrisy isn't there by justifying my anger and decision not to forgive. I can also just completely skip over the tension of praying with first-person plural pronouns, and believe that my relationship with my brother has absolutely nothing to do with God.

In fact, praying for others' provision, pardon, and protection doesn't allow us to embrace hypocrisy by pleading ignorance. Instead, it shapes us into the image of Christ by exposing and purifying us of the many ways we do embrace hypocrisy. God isn't trying to catch us in a trap. He's trying to free us from the traps that are hidden all along the paths of religiosity.

This is what makes the Lord's Prayer supernatural. We don't have the wit and strength to provide for ourselves, let alone for others. Everything we have, including the wit and strength to acquire wealth, comes from God. We can't draw from our own wells of grace in order to pardon others when they offend us. Only from God's bottomless well can we draw what we need to forgive others. We don't have the spiritual fortitude it takes to deny the pleasures of sin and avoid the traps of temptation. We need daily help from the One who gives us everything, forgives us lavishly, and preserves us for all eternity. Jesus teaches us through the Lord's Prayer that we are incredibly needy, and that God is unbelievably generous. When we pray for provision, pardon, and protection for ourselves and each other, we all get to enjoy the feast of God's abundant goodness, which he's so eager to share. His soul food is ours to savor together as a family through prayer.

5

ROOTS

A Family Bred

PREPARING FOR THE WORST

While being interviewed before a boxing match, Mike Tyson was asked for his thoughts on his opponent's style. Tyson observed, "Everyone has a plan until they get punched in the mouth."

Likewise, everyone has a plan for how they'll be victorious until adversity comes. Once disorientation hits, all resolve, strength, and composure vanish like a boxer's two front teeth. Even if you, like me, haven't been in a real fight since the seventh grade, Tyson's words still ring true.

My brother's passing away was the biggest surprise of my life, until it was quickly eclipsed by another surprise just a few weeks later: I was surprised by how much my faith in Jesus and my resolve to stay committed to him vanished. C. S. Lewis's reflections after the death of his wife rang true for me: "God has not been trying an experiment on my faith or love in order to find out their quality. He knew it already. It was I who didn't. . . . He always knew that my temple was a house of cards. His only way of making me realize the fact was to knock it down."[1] I got punched in the face, and my resolve for the Lord disappeared. My strength dried up, and I was left with nothing. Everyone has a plan until they get punched in the mouth.

You're not exempt. You'll get punched. Eventually you'll realize that every single one of us has to deal with adversity. I'm not just referring to the general adversity that comes from life in a fallen world—loved ones dying, chronic illness, death, divorce, loss of a job. I'm talking about the unique suffering that comes to Christians as a result of maintaining faithfulness to God in a fallen world. Willfully following Jesus in this world is like stepping into a boxing ring. Even if you're ultimately victorious, you're setting yourself up for punches that wouldn't have landed had you just stayed out of the ring.

I'm talking about living with prolonged singleness and maybe loneliness because you've resolved to allow Jesus to dictate your sexuality. I'm talking about the loss of a job because you refuse to compromise standards. I'm talking about fighting through depression and anxiety because you refuse to use illegal substances as a temporary escape. The list goes on and on. Sometimes, faithfulness to God puts us in a position where we feel like obedience is a death sentence. In those cases, how will you respond? We'd like to think our temple of faith will withstand the hurricanes, but if our history is any indicator of our present, we know that our house of cards constantly needs to be reinforced.

So how will you prepare for the storm? If we wait to prepare until we're in the middle of a temptation, we're too late. We must be proactive. We need to see the storms coming from afar, and reinforce our walls ahead of time. The strength we need to endure the storm ultimately comes from God, but we take hold of his strength through prayer.

Prayers are our roots. The roots do the hard work of strengthening the tree, but this hard work is hidden work. The same can be said for prayer. Praying together functions as both our actual and ancestral roots. Praying together is both our strength and our heritage as those who suffer a great deal for faithfulness to God.

If the previous chapters taught the standard operating procedure of prayer from the Sermon on the Mount, then Christ's prayer in the garden of Gethsemane offers the magnum opus of how it's done.

YOU'RE NOT AS STRONG AS YOU THINK

In the upper room, Jesus tells his disciples of his impending suffering, but he also tells them the truth about themselves. They'll be cowards and scatter, but Jesus promises not to return the favor. They lack the strength to stand with him, but that's the reason he's going to the cross. They will fail in the future, but those failures have no bearing on his present love and commitment to their good. What a blessing that Christ knows all about our failures, even the ones that haven't happened yet, and yet he remains committed to us.

Jesus then takes his disciples to the garden of Gethsemane, where we see more than Jesus's preaching on prayer; we see his practice of it.

The Place. The garden of Gethsemane was a divine mudroom. Sandwiched between the Last Supper and Jesus's betrayal and arrest, this is where Jesus geared up to face the bitter cold. *Gethsemane* means "the olive press." Pressed olives produced the oil that was used for centuries to anoint kings and priests. Now Jesus stepped into a time of intense pressure for his anointing.

The Partners. While he brought all the disciples to the garden, he asked only Peter, James, and John to come a little farther (Mark 14:33). Why them? Perhaps because they had claimed to have the greatest resolve and strength. James and John earlier said they could drink the same cup that Jesus would drink (10:35–39). Peter had promised to remain faithful even to death (14:29–31). Perhaps Jesus specifically wanted to correct this.

When my infant daughter first came home from the hospital, my two-year-old nephew Jackson did something both cute and condescending. He started speaking to her in baby talk. Baby talk? I explained to Jackson that he is, in fact, a baby. He may know a few words, but he's still in diapers, doesn't cook his own meals, and doesn't have a job. He's a baby just like my daughter. He's not in another league. I think Jesus brought Peter, James, and John along to show them the same thing.

Jesus never wasted an opportunity to train his disciples, even as he faced death. In fact, his sorrow and suffering provided a great backdrop for their training. But Jesus was doing more than just training them. He wanted to feel their support. Jesus, God in the flesh, chose not to do life on earth alone. Even though the disciples couldn't help him drink the cup, he found value in their being with him.

The Posture. As Jesus brought the so-called strongest with him, he didn't share profound words of wisdom. He shared his weakness. He told them, "My soul is very sorrowful, even to death. Remain here and watch" (Mark 14:34). When we pray together, this is exactly what we're doing. We're admitting our weakness and confessing that we must rely on God's strength. This is the right posture for prayer.

Jesus, too, gives us permission to be weak. He primes us to cry out to God in our weakness through his example.

The Pressure. When Jesus says that he came to be a ransom for many (see Mark 10:45), he meant it. He also meant it when he said that he was sorrowful to the point of death. It's an absolutely terrifying thing to stand in front of God and give an account for sin. Meditating on this has driven people into deep depression. Now imagine what it would be like to stand in front of God and pay for the sins of the entire world. God is gracious and merciful, yes! But he doesn't leave the guilty unpunished (see Ex. 34:7). For centuries God had deferred his judgment. But now Jesus would drink this cup of God's wrath down to the dregs.

This is the good news of the gospel for us who have put our faith in him: we don't have to pay for our sins! Jesus drank the full cup of God's wrath for all who put their faith in him. If the whole world were to turn and repent, the whole world would enjoy this gift of salvation. You don't have to pay for your sins—not even one of them! That's good news.

CONFIDENCE AND CONTENTMENT

Jesus had taught his disciples how to pray in times of peace. Here he modeled prayer in the midst of suffering. What had been instructed in the classroom was now illustrated in crisis.

I wouldn't be surprised if Ryle, that old Anglican preacher, had this instance in mind when he said, "Death beds are great revealers of secrets."[2] Jesus stared death square in the eyes, knowing his fate was inescapable. How did he face it? On his knees in prayer. His teaching on prayer was more than theory. It was tested and proven true. This was prayer in its truest and purest form.

Abba: Our Father. When Jesus prays, he refers to God as "Abba" (Mark 14:36). At a time when most of us would think of God as an enemy, Jesus uses this most intimate name for God. He cries out to someone he knows will listen, someone who cares for his well-being. He is not calling out to an employer who's concerned only about the bottom line and will step on his employees to make a profit. He is calling out to his Father who has loved him perfectly from all eternity.

Help: Confidence in God's Ability. Then Jesus cries out, "All things are possible for you. Remove this cup from me" (Mark 14:36). In desperation, this is where prayer begins: knowing that God can do the impossible. There's no prayer without this! And who knows better than Jesus that God can do the impossible?

Recently when reading Sherlock Holmes, I was struck by something his assistant John Watson said. Faced with another impossible case, Watson observed, "So accustomed was I to [Holmes's] invariable success that the very possibility of his failing had ceased to enter into my head."[3] Watson got so used to seeing Sherlock work wonders that he inherently knew Sherlock would do the impossible. So it is with God. A seminary professor of mine would say, "What God has done in the past is a model and a promise of what he will continue to do in the future, although he's too creative to do the same thing the same way twice."[4]

The disciples tended to place God in a box. It's only as they walked with Jesus that their boundaries began to shatter. Water is turned into wine—the boundaries enlarge. The blind see and the lame walk—the boundaries enlarge. Five thousand are fed—the boundaries enlarge again. Lazarus gets up—the boundaries shatter! Jesus was in the business of helping doubters believe, but he himself didn't have any boundaries of doubt. He was aware that God could do the impossible, and so he prayed like it. If anyone could provide another way, it was God!

Hear me. We won't consistently pray if we're not sure of God's ability. So much of our failure to pray comes from subtly believing that within God exists the possibility of failure. Because of this, we never ask God to do the impossible. Instead, we pursue only the things we can accomplish on our own.

Hope: Contentment in God's Activity. Jesus ends his prayer by saying, "Yet not what I will, but what you will" (Mark 14:36). While prayer may start with believing God can do the impossible, peace is never found there. If we only imagine what God can do and then judge his goodness by how often he does the impossible for us, we'll never find true peace. His ability should cause our hearts to soar and ask for the impossible. But his sovereignty and wisdom should keep us grounded. They remind us that although God *can* do the impossible, he doesn't have to—and we can trust him regardless. Peace is found here and only here.

Any other arrangement ends only in discontentment, especially if we hold God hostage to an outcome he's never promised. We'll always lack peace when we judge God's love for us by how many of our prayers are answered with a "yes." False hope is the most fertile soil for a crop of discontentment.

Jesus helps us see that we must surrender our hearts, and surrendering our hearts takes persistence. Gethsemane shows us that Jesus didn't utter these twenty-three words only once and then get up and go on with his mission. He repeated this request over and over. Jesus spent an hour "saying the same words" (Mark 14:39). He was persistent.

There are times that persisting in a particular prayer can be foolish, particularly when we fail to rest in "God's will be done." Still, Jesus shows us that persisting in prayer doesn't reveal a lack of faith. It can be a indicator of great faith. If I were convinced God couldn't do anything or wouldn't do anything, I'd stop asking! Yet persisting in prayer is also how we wrestle our wills into submitting to his. Persistent prayer is our saying, "I know I should want to want your will, but I don't. God, help me want what you want. Help me to run headfirst into obedience."

SURRENDERED HEARTS, STRENGTHENED HANDS

While Jesus struggled in prayer, his disciples fell asleep (see Mark 14:34–40). He had asked them to stay awake and pray (Mark 14:38), linking prayer with the ability to withstand temptation. But they didn't. They had every advantage to pray. They weren't weighed down by the same stress that drove Jesus to sweat drops of blood. Yet they failed this test of faithfulness in the garden, just like Adam and Eve. Their resolve, like ours, wasn't enough.

But Jesus wrestles in prayer. He surrenders his heart to God, and he experiences unimaginable strength to move forward (see Luke 22:43). Through his example, Jesus reminds us that surrendering our hearts to God is the pathway to strengthening our hands.

Have you ever noticed that Jesus doesn't seem to struggle with discerning God's answers to prayers like we do? One of the most difficult and confusing things about prayer, especially persistent prayer, is knowing when God has actually answered. I don't know about you, but I've never heard God speak audibly. Since he doesn't normally speak that way, how do we know when to move forward? It doesn't seem like Jesus hears audibly from God in this moment, yet he is confident in God's answer and resolves to move forward.

Seeing an angry mob approaching, Jesus tells his disciples, "Are you still sleeping and taking your rest? It is enough; the hour has come. The Son of Man is betrayed into the hands of sinners. Rise, let us be going; see, my betrayer is at hand" (Mark 14:41–42). Jesus is teaching us something here: impressions can be misleading, but providence is not. Jesus persisted in praying and training his disciples until a mob came to arrest him (see Luke 22:47). At this point, he knew God had said, "No, there's no other way." Jesus then moved forward into God's will. It wasn't what he asked for, but he doesn't run from it. He knew the safest place to be is in God's will, even if that will meant his death.

Not only does Jesus walk toward God's will but the Gospels

describe Jesus as having an unparalleled resolve and even peace as he faces crucifixion. Jesus agonizes in Gethsemane, but endures the cross. Jesus is smacked in the face, but he doesn't retaliate. A crown of thorns is placed on his head, but he doesn't take it off. He is flogged, but he doesn't call for it to stop. He has enough composure to look at his crying mom and say to John, "Would you take care of my mom? Ma, John's going to be your new son. He'll make sure you're taken care of." While hanging from the cross and choking on the blood filling his lungs, he doesn't use his last breaths to gasp for air and hold on a little longer. He spends those precious breaths giving assurance to a repentant sinner next to him. He spends his last breaths crying out for God's forgiveness for those who haven't yet repented.

What we get is a picture of someone who agonized in prayer overnight and surrendered his heart to do God's will. We get a picture of someone who is granted the strength and resolve to do God's will—even to the point of death. Though our ancestors Adam and Eve failed to submit to God's will in a garden, Jesus didn't. Though Jesus's suffering was unique and never to be repeated, his example provides the template for Christian faithfulness. We strengthen our hands by surrendering our hearts. This is how we move forward with power.

NO ISOLATED INSTANCES

Prayerlessness is a blindfold that makes us unaware of the dangers around us. It gives us a false sense of peace and a naive courage. It leads us to presume that we don't need the Lord's help. The disciples had their night shades on and were sleeping peacefully, while Jesus was staring down the cup of God's wrath. Prayer makes us aware of the dangers that surround us and our inability to fight. But prayer also makes us aware of the Helper who keeps us safe. We feel weak, we know we're incredibly weak, and we realize our safety has absolutely nothing to do with our strength.

The story of Gethsemane is as much about the power of prayer as it is about the inevitable failure that comes from prayerlessness. The episode is sandwiched between the disciples promising faithfulness to Jesus and the disciples running away in fear. It's sandwiched between Peter saying, "I'd die for you," and Peter denying Jesus. Like a vegan sandwich, the disciples present great promise, but they deliver disappointment in the middle.

Jesus's faithfulness to do God's task is directly tied to his prayer. The disciples' faithlessness is directly tied to their prayerlessness. Jesus connects them when he warns the disciples, "Watch and pray that you may not enter into temptation. The spirit indeed is willing, but the flesh is weak" (Mark 14:38).

Three days after Jesus dies on the cross, the disciples are shocked to see him alive again in a resurrected body. When Jesus did what God called him to do, it served as his death sentence. But death wasn't his final destination. And he has promised the same for all those who have put their trust in him: the ability to prayerfully encounter suffering.

We see the disciples embrace Jesus's teaching and example of prayer in the book of Acts. The results are earth-shaking. In Acts 4, Peter and John are unjustly beaten and thrown into jail for preaching the gospel. They suffer for the sake of righteous-ness. God breaks them out of jail. And do you know what they do? They gather with their friends and have a prayer meeting (Acts 4:23–31). And what do they pray? They pray that their sovereign God would give them boldness and strength to do his will.

In Acts 5, they get arrested again, beaten, and ordered not to speak about Jesus. But they leave the scene rejoicing. Yes, rejoicing! And they repeat this over and over (see Acts 5:42). What happened to the sleepy, prayerless disciples in the garden?

They tapped into the power of God through prayer. God strengthened their hands when they surrendered their hearts to do his will. They began to look like their Savior. They fi-nally understood that the life-changing work of the gospel isn't strengthened in the public eye. Rather, it's strengthened in pri-vate before the eyes of God and our family in Christ.

6

GLORY

The Role of Prayer in Corporate Worship

PARTICIPANTS, NOT SEASON TICKET HOLDERS

I thought I hated baseball. I watched it to cure insomnia. Then one day in elementary school, my friends came to the door with aluminum baseball bats and tennis balls. We used the cars and lampposts in our cul-de-sac as bases, and we started playing baseball. And you know what? Baseball wasn't that bad. In fact, baseball was great! It was suddenly engaging and enjoyable. We played for hours, and the time just flew. It wasn't baseball I hated. It was just watching it. What made the difference? Participation. The worth of the sport shouldn't be judged by spectating, but by participating.

Corporate worship—that time and space where the church gathers to worship God—isn't meant to be a spectator sport where people come to take their seats in the stands to be entertained with singing and a funny, relevant message. Unfortunately, too many people attend church like they attend their favorite sports game: as season ticket holders to a spectator sport. But like baseball, corporate worship is meant for participating, not spectating.

Various churches have attempted to make corporate worship more participatory. Some create space for meaningful interaction before and after the service. Some incorporate the introvert's nightmare, better known as the "greet your neighbor" time. Some foster an environment where people speak back and shout during the preaching. Some have removed the preaching altogether, considering monologue the biggest obstacle to participation. The desire to help congregants participate in corporate worship is a good desire. That said, these attempts miss the purpose of our corporate gathering.

We gather to meet with God together. God has always intended that we would know him better through our engagement with others, but we don't want our engagement with others to eclipse engaging with God. So it's crucial that God's Word remain central to our gathering. We hear the Word preached, sang, and read. And in response, we pray. We gather to meet with him together in large part through prayers that are responses to his Word.

WHAT DOES IT LOOK LIKE TO PRAY TOGETHER?

If we know prayer is designed to foster participation in our meeting with God, it's important to examine just how we should pray together. Corporate prayer is a way we teach our church how to engage with God. When we pray together, we want to address misconceptions about God, pray for those things many of us neglect, and show that substantial prayer doesn't have to take a substantial amount of time.

We can't assume people know how to pray. This is why we vary the prayers we use from week to week. Four types of prayer are modeled and commanded in Scripture, and these should shape our corporate prayer time. I don't think any of these four types of prayers will be new to you. If you have any experience in a church, you've heard of the ACTS model of prayer: adoration, confession, thanksgiving, and supplication. While it may not be novel, using some combination of these prayers in corporate worship is necessary to create a participatory environment where people worship God together.

ADORATION: DO YOU KNOW WHO YOU'RE TALKING TO?

"Do you know who you're talking to? You must know who I am!" I heard this countless times in my younger years. It usually came when I said something out of line or acted extracasual with my teacher, coach, or some other authority figure. It can be a statement of rebuke, but it can also be an encouragement. I remember approaching my mom from time to time to ask for forgiveness for ways I offended her. I'd come with timidity, and she would so graciously respond, "Don't you know who you're talking to?" It was a rhetorical question meant to remind me who she was—a loving mother. Remembering her character would be the antidote to my trepidation. Similarly, this is what our prayers of adoration are designed to do.

The prayer of praise sets the foundation of our time together. Yet it's often left out of our corporate prayers. In our church, the prayer of adoration typically comes first. We want to establish in our hearts that it's an honor to speak to God. Familiarity with God is a gift, but familiarity can quickly turn into flippancy. This prayer reminds us who we're talking to. Before we call out to God to fulfill his covenant promises, we need to be reminded that we're talking to a promise-keeping God. Because of Jesus's great sacrifice, we can come boldly to God. But we should also come humbly.

In our prayers of praise, we want to remember what God is like, not just what he's done for us. We're praising him for his attributes and characteristics—his holiness, gentleness, goodness, even his wrath. The wonder of these prayers doesn't come simply from listing off God's attributes, but from unpacking them. A prayer of adoration at the beginning of the service helps blow away the clouds of moderate affection and boredom.

One Christmas, my wife got a present from a dear friend. The box sat under our tree for about a week. As she examined the giftwrapped box, she didn't have strong positive or negative feelings about it. Yet the moment she opened the package and saw the gift, tears of joy poured down her cheeks. What changed? When the contents of the box were unpacked, she saw the true nature of what was inside and couldn't hold back the tears.

This is what we do in the prayer of praise. We unpack the character of God accurately, meticulously, even imaginatively. The fog of lethargy dissipates, and joy-filled worship permeates our gathering.

We should desire to praise God not generally, but specifically. This helps to minimize the empty phrases people tend to use. It also fills in the gaps where people tend to import their own definitions of God. For example, we praise God for his eternality. Because he exists from everlasting to everlasting, he is God (see Ps. 90:2). He's been on the throne forever. He has witnessed the birth of every evil ruler. He remembers them as babies. He knows the day they'll be buried. He's never intimidated. They'll come and go, but he will remain on the throne. His position is secure. He never makes a decision out of fear that someone will take his place. His back is never against a wall, which means we can trust he has no ulterior motives for giving us the commands he does. We better understand all of this eternality during a prayer of adoration.

Delving into God's attributes means we must pay attention to the attributes of God we sometimes feel tempted to apologize for. It shows us we should adore them. Think of God's anger and wrath. When we praise him for those things during corporate worship, we're reminded that God is committed to justice. Wrath isn't a liability. It's proof of his protection. God's anger, directed at sin, reminds us that he is a protector of the weak. His inability to ignore sin and the relentless way he punishes evil is scary because we fear we could easily find ourselves as the objects of his wrath. But for those who take shelter under the protection he has offered through his Son, we realize God's holiness is for our protection, not our punishment.

Do you know who you're talking to? I'm not convinced everyone who comes to corporate worship does. Even if we do know, we forget. Thankfully, prayers of adoration remind us.

CONFESSION: ME TOO!

If we do adoration right, then confession becomes the reflex of our souls. As we reflect on God's holiness and goodness, our sinfulness becomes apparent. As we reflect on God's grace and forgiveness through Christ, we're led to confess.

Genesis 3 wasn't a rewrite of God's original script in order to create more drama throughout the rest of the Bible. It was written to set the stage for God's plan to forgive sinners. When Moses asks to see God's glory, the first thing God testifies about himself is that he is a forgiving God (see Ex. 34:6–7). He doesn't need to be coerced into forgiving. It's his idea. He has made provision both for the guilty to be punished and for his people to experience forgiveness—all of it without compromising his holiness. He did this through Jesus, our substitute (see Rom. 3:21–26). God's offer of forgiveness encourages forthrightness with our flaws. Think of the prodigal son who, "when he came to himself," remembered the generous nature of his father (Luke 15:17–19). The father's kindness compelled the son to return and confess his sin.

When we hear members of our church family confess their sin, we should think to ourselves, "Me too." We often minimize sin in our lives, while maximizing it in the lives of others. But as we hear others confess their sin, we begin to see how the things we overlooked this past week were really worse than we thought. We're reminded of how much we've put our hope in other things for our joy. We're forced to sit, listen, and have our memories jogged enough to say, "Me too! Me too! Me too! And I've done worse than what they've said."

A community that routinely confesses sin together is a community that is glad, growing, gracious, and grounded.

Glad Community. Confession is designed to produce worship, but because it challenges us to explore the darkness of our hearts, we often forsake it. Far from leading us to despair, confession should actually lead us to joy. God's faithfulness and goodness shines especially bright against the backdrop of our failures. Psalms 32 and 51, two popular psalms of repentance, are also beautiful expressions of rejoicing in the forgiveness of God. After the psalmist confesses, this once guilt-ridden sinner calls on everyone he knows to get in on this forgiveness he's found in God (see Ps. 32:11; 51:14).

Now multiply that experience by all the members of your church. Can you imagine the joy?

Growing Community. Repenting together is also a great motivator toward evangelism. Psalm 130 gives us a perfect picture of this. In verses 1–6, the psalmist cries to God for help, receives that help, and puts his hope in God's Word. Verses 7–8 reveal his response to God's help. Now the psalmist wants the whole nation to experience God's forgiveness and love. God's forgiveness is too good to keep to ourselves, and it's too true not to apply to everyone else. When forgiveness is experienced corporately through confession, the gospel message is personally applied *and* publicly announced. A community that freely confesses their sins together is eager to share about the outcome of that freedom with others. This community beckons a dying world, "Come. Taste and see the same forgiveness we're tasting and seeing."

Gracious Community. As we've already seen in the Lord's Prayer, you can't shout about God's forgiveness if you're stingy with your own. A community of people who confess their sins together is constantly reminded that they themselves are sinners who daily need God's forgiveness. So we not only give space and understanding when sinned against, but we also expect it. We're reminded that our apology wasn't a prerequisite for God's offer of forgiveness. Therefore, we shouldn't require an apology for our offering forgiveness to those who sin against us. Jealousy, strife, and competition are driven away as we confess our sins together. A prayerful community of confession is a peaceful community.

Grounded Community. Confession brings everyone down to earth. We realize that if we're really at rock bottom, it's impossible to treat anyone in a condescending manner. As we're led in prayers of confession by the most "respectable" among us, no one feels the need to perform. When leaders in the church confess their weaknesses, the members don't see their own weaknesses as something strange or disqualifying. Prayers of confession remind Christians with weaker consciences that no temptation has overtaken them that isn't common to all people, including the people they look up to most. Corporate confession levels the playing field, which provides a great testimony to both Christian and non-Christian alike.

THANKSGIVING: WHY ME?

Through the prayer of adoration we remember God has no obligation to do anything good for any of us. Through the prayer of confession, we remember God has done for us exactly what he isn't obligated to do. He has created us, cared for us, provided for us, forgiven us, adopted us—the list goes on. He's kind to all of his creation in so many ways. But he is especially kind to his children. He sits in the heavens and does what he pleases, and he is pleased to do good to us despite our sin. That gives us every reason to praise him.

The only proper response to grace is gratitude. But we often respond to grace with entitlement, which is seen most clearly in our grumbling. The best way to see if your heart is filled with gratitude or entitlement is to consider what you mean when you ask the question, "Why me?" The entitled heart asks, "Why me?" and means, "God, why didn't you answer my prayers the way I wanted you to?" But the humble heart asks, "Why me?" and means, "God, why have you been so good to me? I don't deserve you or any of your gifts." Taking the time to thank God together for specific things he has done for us should foster hearts of humility and gratitude. Through the prayer of thanksgiving, we who grumble are called to count our blessings and be reminded that we have it better than we deserve. And it's all thanks to God.

This time of thanksgiving is vital to our Sunday gathering because a broken spirit can be a great obstacle to hearing God's gracious words (see Ex. 6:9). A penny can block our view of the shining sun if we hold it close enough to our eyes. Likewise, our problems can blind us to the glory of God if we dwell on them enough.

I sometimes consider God's omnipotence, and then consider all that's still broken in this world and my life, and I grumble. But when I witness my brothers and sisters giving thanks to God despite (and even for) the various hardships in their lives, my heart is redirected to gratitude and joy. We should desire as a church to be sorrowful at what is wrong in this world, yet always rejoicing because of God's character and promises (see 2 Cor. 6:10). A prayer of thanksgiving lets the brightness of God's glory outshine our penny-sized problems.

85

INTERCESSION/SUPPLICATION: WE NEED YOUR HELP!

Having prayed all of the above, we're reminded that God is glorified when we lean on him. He cares for those who make him their refuge (Nah. 1:7). So much burdens us, especially in this day and age of social media. Our personal problems are compounded with the world's problems. Social media comes in and asks, "Did you hear about . . . another instance of police brutality . . . another law passed that demonizes Christian values . . . another polarizing election . . . another Christian leader's moral failure . . . another martyr . . . another miscarriage . . . another friend diagnosed with cancer?" The list goes on and on. While we don't want to shy away from conversations about these things, we want to begin conversation with the One who sits above us. The prayer of supplication during corporate worship allows us to unburden ourselves to God.

At my church, our members lead us in prayers of adoration, confession, and thanksgiving. As pastors, we've decided to lead the prayer of supplication. We do this in order to broaden the horizon of what our community believes we can request of God. In this domesticated and tame era of Christianity, we recognize that people tend to be pretty narrow in what they ask for. We want to show that it's okay to ask God for things like healing. It's okay to persistently pray the same prayer. It's okay to ask God for things without always saying, "If it's in your will, God." Of course, we want our hearts to desire God's will above all else. But many of us doubt God's ability and desire to do great things in our lives. We want to put the greatness of Jesus on display by asking for big things in his name. Sometimes, in his providence, God answers "no"—and through that we grow together. But we've also made great requests of God and seen him respond above and beyond all we could ask or think. Either way, our faith is strengthened as a family when together we ask God for his help.

PUTTING IT INTO PRACTICE

You may see the necessity and benefit of all of these prayers, but you may be asking, "How do I put all this into practice during a church service?" Here are three guidelines that may help.

First, fostering an environment of participation doesn't mean excluding leadership. Churches not accustomed to working through these four prayers in their weekly services need leaders to set the example and teach. This is not a private prayer. It's leading the whole church to pray together. So pastors should be mindful of the character and competence of the people they ask to lead these prayers.

Second, those leading prayers publicly should ordinarily spend time beforehand in preparation. While you don't want people to read an essay and call it a prayer, you also don't want them to wing it. Preparation keeps people from rambling and from thoughtless repetition. It helps people to pray substantively, conscientiously, sensitively, pointedly. It serves everyone participating through listening by keeping them interested. Engaging with God requires focus, thoughtfulness, and clarity. Help the people praying to consider the weight of what they're preparing to do: leading God's people to worship him.

Third, slow down. We're not in a rush. Prayer is a vital part of the service that can't be skipped over or zipped through.

VARIED COMMUNICATION

As a church, we want worship to be corporate. We want to showcase a variety of God's people speaking to God in various ways. We want our community and our visitors to see that significant prayer can happen in various forms in a short period of time. All of this is possible when prayer is emphasized in our Sunday gathering.

Our God wants a deep relationship with his people. And the deeper the relationship, the more varied the communication. We explore the wonder of who God is during our prayer of adoration. We embrace the mercy he provides during our prayer of confession. We reflect on all he's done for us during our prayer of thanksgiving. We lean on him and feel his strength during our prayer of supplication. By including these prayers in our Sunday service, we display the width and depth of our relationship with God.

Early in my pastorate, I visited a church that lacked most of my stylistic preferences, including its music and preaching style. But they prayed like I described in this chapter. Prayer played a major role in their service. I'd never experienced a sense of participation from the pews like I did in that service. I didn't leave feeling merely like I received something, but like I participated in something, namely, worship. This church asked me to participate and engage with God alongside his people. It was like baseball. What might have bored me as a spectator, captured me as a participant. We taste God's glory in a unique way as we participate together in corporate worship through prayer.

7

LEAN ON ME

The Role of Prayer in Corporate Care

LEANING OR LEARNING

The year was 1992. I was eight years old and had just finished watching the Summer Olympics. I'd decided I was going to be a gymnast when I grew up. But first things first: I had to learn how to do a backflip. I went to my school's library, deciphered the mystery that was the Dewey Decimal System, and found a book on gymnastics. I flipped to the section that talked about back handsprings, read it repeatedly, and examined the diagrams. After school, I got my mattress from upstairs, brought it to the front lawn, and attempted my first back handspring.

Fast-forward a few frames, and now see me limping away humbled. Apparently, back handsprings are easier read than done. I had to practice. I had to learn how to depend on my hands to support the weight of my body as I turned over backward in midair.

As it turns out, you can't learn (or teach) dependence didactically. Dependence isn't gained by learning, but by leaning. Just as I couldn't learn how to do a backflip by reading books, you can't teach a church to depend on God by propositions alone. Practice is necessary, and that practice is prayer. A church that practices prayer is more than a church that learns; it's also a church that leans. It's more than a church that knows; it's also a church that feels. We learn dependence by leaning on God together.

FORCED TO LEAN

Our church was forced to lean. The suffering early on in the life of our church made dependence on God tangible. Our first nine months weren't full of weddings, births, new members, and conversions. The excitement that characterizes many church plants filled with a bunch of twenty- and thirty-somethings was nowhere to be found. Instead, it was as dreary as a Seattle winter. In March, a church member experienced the death of her mother figure and mentor. In April, my brother died. In May, another church member lost his sister to cancer. On June 7, 2015, the day our church actually launched, we received news that my wife's grandmother had just passed away.

The same rang true for July, August, September, and October. There were some high notes, like the October baptism of a fifty-three-year-old church member whose diagnosis of cancer was used by God to awaken her to her sin disease. But on January 30, 2016, this same cancer that introduced her to Jesus snatched her from us and gave her a face-to-face meeting with her Savior. We rejoiced when we baptized her, and we mourned when we buried her just a few months later.

Life had crippled us. Joy was elusive. Sorrow was near. We were forced to learn what it meant to lean on God as we cared for one another. We didn't have words of wisdom, or adequate resources to care for everyone's needs. We were ill-equipped to deal with the burdens we had committed to carry. Through it all, we learned one lesson: when life knocks you down to your knees, don't be so quick to get up. Instead, be quick to look to God in prayer. In the school of affliction, we learned to lean.

My question for you is this: Where do people actually learn to lean on God in your church? Is there a space for them to learn dependence? Is there a time set aside? Or is it assumed that people will take the instructions and diagrams laid out during the preaching and work out the dependence part on their own? Thankfully, we aren't expected to be innovators. We don't have to come up with new strategies or plans to help people learn what it means to lean on God. We only need to be investigators of what God has already laid out. Even if we look in a cursory manner at God's Word, we'll see the solution is right under our noses.

FOCUS ON THE OBVIOUS

One of the most important lessons I learned when it came to Bible study is captured in the acronym FOTO: Focus On The Obvious. Our first step in Bible study should be to look for the things that are plain to any reader. Don't start with a magnifying glass. Start with an aerial shot. To understand the importance of prayer in the life of the church, one only needs to fly over the book of Acts.

To be clear, details are important. All of the Bible is inspired by God, and God carefully chose those who wrote it. Luke, the physician who wrote both Luke and Acts, was meticulous in giving a detailed and orderly account of the life of Jesus (see Luke 1:1–4) and the beginning of the church (see Acts 1:1–3). He wanted his audience to be certain about the things he had learned.

Luke characterizes the church as a people of prayer. Even a cursory reading of the book of Acts shows us the prevalence of corporate prayer.

- The disciples pray together generally and for wisdom in establishing another leader to take the place of Judas. (1:12–26)
- The church constantly prays together as the general rhythm of their lives. (2:42–47)
- Peter and John (together) go up to the temple during the hour of prayer. (3:1)
- The church prays for boldness in the face of opposition. (4:23–31)
- The church prays for the blessing of the selected leaders. The apostles stay devoted to corporate prayer. (6:1–6)
- Stephen, the first martyr, prays for the forgiveness of those who are killing him. (7:59–60)
- Peter and John pray together with the saints in Samaria that they might receive the Holy Spirit. (8:14–15)
- Peter commands Simon to repent and to pray that the intent of his heart would be forgiven, and Simon asks Peter to join him. (8:22–24)
- Peter prays and sees a woman rise from the dead. (9:40)
- Cornelius prays continually to the Lord, and God gives him direction for salvation. (10:1–8)
- Peter follows his prayer regimen, and God confronts his personal prejudices and limited view of God. (10:9–23)
- The church prays together for Peter's deliverance. (12:1–5)
- Peter is delivered and comes to a prayer meeting. (12:12)

- The church fasts and prays for God to multiply his work. (13:1–3)
- Paul and Barnabas appoint elders and commit them to the Lord through prayer and fasting. (14:23)
- Paul, Silas, and Luke collectively go to a place of prayer. (16:16)
- Paul and Silas pray together in jail. (Nothing can stop these brothers from praying together.) (16:25)
- Paul prays together with the pastors as he gets ready to leave a church. (20:36)
- Paul prays with the family of God before he sets sail to Jerusalem. This would ultimately be the trip where his resolve to die for Christ would be put to the test. (Acts 20:24; 21:1–14)
- Luke, Paul, and the crew of the ship pray together as they fear being shipwrecked. (27:29)
- Paul prays for the healing of a man suffering from dysentery. He's healed, and the rest of the people on the island come for healing. (28:8–9)

See what I mean? Prayer is mentioned no less than twenty-one times in Acts. Furthermore, these prayers are inherently corporate. Whenever prayer is mentioned, it overwhelmingly involves others. Even in instances when individuals are praying, they involve interpersonal relationships (e.g., Stephen prays for his murderers to be forgiven and thus included in God's family; Peter and Cornelius are brought together through their private prayers). Luke highlights that the church did more than learn truths about God. They really leaned on him. In Acts, Christians regularly gathered for prayer. Why is it that this kind of prayer is absent in many of our churches today?

RECOVERING THE PRAYER MEETING

While the previous chapter discussed praying when we gather to worship, I want to examine the other side of the coin here. There should be routine times in the lives of our churches when we gather for the sole purpose of praying. This is different from praying during corporate worship, but it's just as necessary. Prayer during corporate worship is the potatoes to the steak of the preached Word. In the prayer meeting, the roles are reversed. Now our prayer with one another becomes the main dish. We care for each other best as we lean on God together.

I know the idea of a prayer meeting doesn't sound very glamorous. The trouble is, churches and pastors feel the pressure of innovation constantly. Our society is obsessed with innovation, so the common and plain are regularly devalued. People want something fresh, new, and exciting. Pastors like me are tempted to think we need to create exciting events that people will want to attend. Yet prayer meetings are seldom exciting. People come into a room, share their burdens with each other, and together take them before God with eyes closed and heads bowed.

The truth is, we don't need to innovate. We only need to be intentional. The prayer meeting isn't meant to be a theme park. It's more like a storage facility, and we're all cars without trunks. We were never meant to store up our concerns within ourselves (see Ps. 13:2). We were meant to off-load those things to God. The prayer meeting isn't a place of attraction, but a place of necessity. It's a place where people come with burdens and leave without them because they've been placed in God's hands. Here, we come together to lean on God with each other, for the sake of each other. Where's that space for your church?

NEW RESPONSIBILITY, NEW RUBRIC

Establishing or recovering a consistent prayer meeting does at least two things for a church: (1) It reinforces our sense of responsibility for one another, and (2) it provides a new rubric to use when evaluating how well we're carrying each other's burdens and sorrows.

As we weep with those who weep and rejoice with those who rejoice (Rom. 12:15), we're reminded that we're part of a family. We're reminded that each of us possesses a bigger identity. The "I" has become a "we." No longer are we individuals consumed with our own worlds. We're interdependent parts of a body called to give thanks together and grieve together. Our joys and sufferings are no longer merely personal and confidential; they're meant to be felt vicariously. Everyone in the community is called to experience the joys of God's goodness in the lives of others while simultaneously inhaling the secondhand smoke of each other's hard times. As family, we come together to share these things, and then take them to God in both praise and petition.

Praying together also gives us a new rubric for defining success. We aren't God. We aren't omnipotent. We can't change things. We're not omniscient, so our knowledge to counsel others is limited. And we aren't omnipresent, so we're limited in our ability to be with people in their hard times. We know all this, yet when we're aware of the increasing problems in the lives of our church family, we get so easily deflated. When we hear of an unpredicted infidelity, an unexpected cancer, an unimaginable death, or an unavoidable accident, it's so easy to think of what we "should have done" or "could have done." We know we're not God, but that doesn't stop us from feeling guilty about it.

This is where the new rubric comes in. Success isn't defined by how well we prevent tragedies. In our prayers, we praise the One who is omnipotent, omniscient, and omnipresent. Our prayers remind those in need that we have access to this amazing God. They free us from the misguided burden of being God as we take these requests to God himself.

Of course, all that could be seen as an excuse. A cop-out. Life is hard, and we won't be able to carry other burdens perfectly. So why bother?

Have you ever noticed that, in the book of Ruth, everyone who asks God to do something for someone else actually ends up being used by God to do the very thing they prayed for (Ruth 1:9; 3:1–4; 2:12, 15–18; 4:13)? Praying together isn't meant to frustrate our work, but to fuel our work by making us more concerned with one another's lives. Prayer knits our hearts to others in need and increases our concern and eagerness to serve.

RUNNING A PRAYER MEETING

Let's spend a bit of time on the nuts and bolts of actually running a prayer meeting. These are just suggestions and lessons learned by our church as we've sought to cultivate a culture of praying together. We planted our church two years ago, but we began meeting together for corporate prayer a year earlier. So, for the past three years we've gathered together at least once a month for a prayer meeting.

Below are some thoughts on how meeting together to pray has helped us care for our church. I hope they will help you consider how you can approach prayer meetings in your church. This list isn't ranked by order of importance; it's merely a collection of thoughts.

Schedule a prayer meeting. Find a time that works well for your church. We started to do them once a month on Sunday nights from 5 p.m. to 7 p.m. Then we realized that in a church full of young couples with young kids, that was the worst time for a prayer meeting. After a year, we tried a more suitable time.

Remove anything that would compete for people's time. Prayer is a tough discipline to learn, so we want to remove any distractions. We shut down small groups on the first Wednesday of the month so no other church function competes with our prayer time. We provide food and childcare so people don't have to worry about cooking and finding babysitters. We throw a lot of our budget at our prayer time. We want its importance to be reflected in the great pains we'll go to to get everyone there. Right now, we meet once a month, but our goal is to move toward praying as a church more than once a month. We want to constantly grow in the prominence we give to this time.

Begin with the Word. When we gather on Sundays, the preached Word is the steak. This is not that time. Still, the Word is a vital part of what we're trying to do. So we begin with a five- to fifteen-minute encouragement from God's Word, and that serves as the basis for prayer that evening. When writing this chapter, I received a text message from a new member at our church who was impacted by the concept of the role of Scripture in our praying together. She wrote: "Praying through Scripture has been really helpful. Not only are my prayers deeper, but there is more assurance in them, more revelation of God's character, the centrality of Christ, and the work of the Spirit. It leads me to repentance instead of rebellion, and to conviction instead of condemnation. It's so easy to replace God's voice with my own, but when reading through Scripture and praying that back to God, that happens so much less." She's learning to lean on Scripture, not in propositions but in practice. That's the goal!

Populate the prayer list primarily with kingdom, whole body, and major life concerns. Prayer meetings become tedious and unproductive when they turn into long lists of health concerns, particularly of people who aren't members of the church. "Can we pray for my neighbor's upcoming gall bladder surgery?" Therefore, I find it useful to make sure all the prayer requests come through me or whoever is leading the meeting beforehand. Sometimes I even tell people that I'd be happy to pray for them then and there, and that they might raise the concern with their small group, but that we're trying to use the church meeting for something different. We're trying to use it primarily for kingdom concerns, whole body concerns, and major life concerns. Then we use the meeting to walk through my preplanned list.

When populating the list, include praises and petitions. "Rejoice with those who rejoice, weep with those who weep"

(Rom. 12:15) is a great outline for prayer meetings. Look out for encouraging stories in your church. Praise what you want to see more of. Pray for the success of mission in your church members' lives. This helps the church know that God is the one who brings these opportunities, not us. We'll talk more about this in the next chapter.

We also want to petition God for kingdom and major life concerns like health, jobs, resources, success of adoptions, and evangelistic opportunities. We'll spend time praying for family members to get saved, cancer to be healed, coworkers to come to faith, and struggles with infertility. This creates a wave of empathy and care that extends far beyond people's personal relationships. This gives people the tools to fulfill their covenant to care for each other's souls.

The prayer list—not the Sunday service elements, not the preaching style, not even the ethnic makeup of the leadership of the church—is often where the battle for diversity is won or lost. What makes the prayer list is often a reflection of who's praying and whose problems are seen as real, relevant, and important. A friend of mine was a part of a church that refused to pray for anything related to Mike Brown, Trayvon Martin, Alton Sterling, Eric Gardner, Laquawn McDonald, or any other African-American who was killed at the hands of law enforcement, because those issues were "too politicized" and would cause division in their church. This frustrated her. She didn't want her church to march on Washington or hang a Black Lives Matter flag from the steeple. She simply wanted them to pray corporately on these matters because she knew they were deeply significant to many of the minorities in the church.

That church failed to realize something that was apparent to the early church: fostering unity in diversity involves more than including cultural elements in a Sunday service; it involves showing solidarity with minorities in the struggles they face. In Acts 6, the Greek widows were passed over in the distribution for food. The Twelve gather "the full number of the disciples" and establish a churchwide search to name the first proto-deacons (Acts 6:2). The church then chooses seven men with Greek names. In Acts 15, the church champions the inclusion of the Gentiles into God's covenant family by not requiring them to be Jewish. Both events were marked by discussion and prayer that included the concerns of minorities.

The battle for diversity is still won or lost here today. Diversity is more about priorities than programs. And a church prays for what it prioritizes. Your prayer lists essentially serve as price tags on current events and church concerns—assigning value or diminishing it. Therefore, don't populate the prayer list in isolation. Populate the list with the concerns of all the flock. The honorable strides toward diversity are maximized when we pray together to our Father who has no favorite children (see Acts 10:34).

Lastly, we include things on our prayer list that the church should never take for granted. If you use crutches for a long time, you can sometimes forget you're using something to hold your weight. The same is true with leaning on God for his provision. He is faithful. If we don't remind ourselves of this, it's easy to think we're upholding ourselves by our own power.

So we pray for the same things at every meeting to remind our church of our priorities and how we lean on God for them. We pray that God would keep us tethered to his Word. We pray he wouldn't let us attribute our growth to anything but his sovereign kindness. We pray that he will provide for our needs as a church. We ask him to make us a welcoming environment for visitors, and to help us love all of our neighbors without partiality. We ask for boldness in our evangelism and fruit from conversions. The particulars vary from month to month, but these requests remain constant.

Call on people to pray, but don't let them pray too long. We want as many people to participate in these prayers as possible. We want to show people just how easy it is to pray for others. It doesn't take long. In fact, long prayers in prayer meetings can often kill the momentum. We aren't heard for our many words, and that's a good thing. I think Jesus teaches us in Matthew 6 that our prayers are measured by their strength, not their length. Plus, if you have twenty people praying for twenty requests, and everyone prays for five minutes, that's an hour and a half of prayer. Charles Spurgeon gives us words of wisdom about the notorious long pray-er:

> And don't hesitate to tell good Mr. Snooks that, with God's help, he shall not pray for twenty-five minutes. Earnestly entreat him to cut it short, and if he doesn't, then stop him. If a man came into my house intending to cut my wife's throat, first I would reason with him regarding the wrong of it, and then I would effectually prevent him from doing her any harm. I love the church almost as much as I love my dear wife. So, if a man wants to pray long, he can pray long somewhere else but not at the

meeting over which I'm presiding. If he can't pray publicly for a reasonable length of time, tell him to finish it up at home.[1]

Remember the main ingredients. Don't judge success by numbers. You need only two ingredients to start a successful prayer meeting: burdens, and brothers and sisters who are willing to pray. You don't need anyone's permission. Whether you're a pastor or member, you have the ability to model dependence on the Lord in a way that no one would object. You hear a problem? Hurl a prayer. Ask people to pray with you. You have everything you need. Make it a habit to end each conversation with the question, "How can I pray for you?" and then pray for the person right there on the spot, or pray later if time doesn't allow. By doing this you'll see that not all prayer meetings must be scheduled.

PERMISSION TO LEAVE THINGS UNDONE

Gathering to pray helps us embrace our responsibility to each other while allowing us to be content with our limitations. We're no one's saviors. Prayer allows us to leave things unfinished in the lives of people. We realize we're not God, and we don't have the ability to bring immediate resolutions to problems. God is the only one who can calm the raging storms with one word. We can't. We can speak God's Word, and then rely on him to do what only he can do. We admit this when we pray.

When leaving a church that he played an intricate part in nurturing for three years, the apostle Paul pulls the pastors aside and tells them, in a nutshell, "I'm leaving. Wolves are coming, but I'm not the answer to your future problems. You should lean on God and his Word. Let's pray. See you later!" (see Acts 20:25–38). Prayer gives us permission to leave problems unsolved and people undone, for the time being, without feeling as if we've failed them. Praying for someone isn't a cop-out from truly helping them. It's often the most we can do in the moment. In fact, praying for someone is loving because we put them in the hands of the one who can solve any problem. God has promised to finish his work in our lives. As we fervently and frequently come together to pray, we ask God to come through on this precious promise, and we rest knowing he absolutely will.

8

DOING THE RIGHT THING

The Role of Prayer in Missions

DISCONTENTMENT LEADS TO DOING SOMETHING

The year was 1997. Legend has it that a man named Reed Hastings was on his way back from settling a debt with a heartless creditor when an idea for a new business came upon him. The cruel creditor? Blockbuster Video (remember those?). The offense? Apparently, Hastings was charged forty dollars for losing the VHS cassette (remember those?) of *Apollo 13*. Frustrated and disheartened by the corrupt bureaucracy of the video renting industry, he decided it was time someone did something about it. His discontentment led him to fight for the liberation and freedom of video renters everywhere.

And so he came up with Netflix, a service that lets you keep videos for as long as you want without late fees.[1] Hastings took his frustrating circumstance and turned it into gold (so to speak). I say "legend has it" because the authenticity of this story has been contested.[2] Though it may or may not be true, it makes for a great point: discontentment often leads us to action.

While every church has something to be discontent about, the most common discontentment involves getting church members to live missionally. For the sake of establishing a baseline, let's just use the word *evangelism* as we talk about our corporate mission. Evangelism means getting our people out of the pews to share the gospel so that others can get into the pews on their way to heaven. Trying to encourage Christians toward evangelism has been one of the most difficult endeavors in my time as a pastor. My discontentment with this situation has led me to try to do something about it.

When it comes to training Christians for our corporate mission, we often assume people just need more training, more knowledge, more apologetics, more motivation, and a little bit more guilt. There's no shortage of evangelism programs, books on how to properly evangelize, or Facebook ads that guarantee church growth. Some of these efforts are helpful. However, I don't think the main obstacle to evangelism is competence, which means the best fix isn't just more training. To be sure, training is a part of the solution, but if you've come from a background like mine, then you've sat in churches with some pretty competent people but little evangelistic activity.

If our main problem were competence, then evangelism training programs wouldn't constantly need to be updated, reinvented, and innovated. Even after being competently trained, insecurity always seeps back in, doesn't it? Moses met God at the burning bush, he was equipped with a handful of miracles, and he still felt like he wasn't ready. Unlike Moses, the woman at the well was a great evangelist with very little experience (see John 4). The need for more training is often a good excuse for cowards like me to stay away from the task of evangelism. Misidentifying a problem will lead us to doing something, but it won't lead us to doing the right thing.

THE PROBLEM: ANXIETY AND APATHY

When someone becomes a Christian, it's not long before he realizes he has work to do. He's obligated to share his faith with others so that they too can become Christians. He realizes he plays a role in helping others become Christians. But the command to spread the gospel comes with a tension that's difficult to resolve. Here it is: God is sovereign, but he calls me to evangelize. God alone saves, but I'm supposed to share the gospel so people will be saved.

So is this God's work or mine? People tend to lean one of two ways because of this tension. They lean toward anxiety because they'll mess up, or apathy because God will save whomever he wants to save.

Anxiety: Crushing

Many Christians are filled with anxiety when they think of having to "convert" other people to Christianity. They rightly understand they have a responsibility, so they focus on everything they have to do. But they wrongly assume *they* have to produce the results, which leads them to being so consumed by the burden of people's salvation that they freeze and end up not sharing the gospel at all. The fear of failure yields forfeit. As I once heard a preacher say, "Closed mouths lead to an open hell."[3]

This anxiety can also lead Christians to try to manufacture

and manipulate converts. They share the gospel in a way people will accept rather than a way they'll understand. Or they don't share it all. This may look like scheduled "revivals," guilt trips, baptizing kids in fire trucks, or even removing offensive parts of the gospel. Anxious Christians either don't share *at* all or they don't share *it* all.

Anxiety is crushing. We're carrying weight we were never meant to carry. This anxiety keeps us from speaking on behalf of God, and it keeps us from persisting. When we don't get the results we want, it reinforces our anxiety. In Exodus 5:22–23, Moses comes back from what appeared to be an unsuccessful attempt at an exodus, and he asks God, "O Lord, why have you done evil to this people? Why did you ever send me? For since I came to Pharaoh to speak in your name, he has done evil to this people, and you have not delivered your people at all." Like Moses, our anxiety leads us to ask, "Why did I care so much? Why did you put this burden on my back?"

Apathy: Cruising

Apathy is another wrong response when it comes to our call to participate in God's mission. People tend toward laziness in evangelism when they neglect their responsibility in favor of embracing the truth that God is sovereign in salvation. They wrongly believe evangelism somehow becomes inconsequential because God is in control.

Apathy comes from the desire to avoid responsibility. It's an attempt to cruise through life burden-free. Concern for people's souls is a burden that should lead us to tears (see Rom. 10:1–4). An old mentor of mine used to say, "There's no smaller package than a man wrapped up in himself." There's no lighter package either. When a love for self crowds out our ability to love others, we're only willing to carry our own weight.

If Moses offered the biblical case for anxiety, Jonah offered the biblical test case for apathy. His rationale at the end of the book showed that he had a self-love that crowded out his ability to love others. God could awaken a response from Jonah only by attacking his comfort. Jonah was largely unconcerned about the implications of salvation for anyone other than himself and the people he loved (his nation). When faced with an opportunity to participate in God's mission, he chose to fall back. It wasn't his problem to begin with. He could see only the potential negative outcomes. He thought, "What will happen to me if I go?"

Moses and Jonah show us that biblical knowledge left unapplied isn't enough. If anxiety is like being crushed in a car because you loaded a boulder on top of it, then apathy is like putting the car on cruise control and falling asleep behind the wheel. In their action and inaction, the anxious and the apathetic ultimately fulfill the work of Satan. They're either providing people a false sense of security through an insufficient gospel (see Matt. 7:21–24), or they're failing to present the message that will save others (see Ezek. 3:18). Either way, Satan is pleased. What do we do with these two great enemies to our corporate mission? What's the next step?

THE REMEDY: PRAYING TO A SOVEREIGN GOD

Prayer is the link in the chain that connects God's sovereignty to our responsibility. We can try to ease our discontentment by doing something, or we can do the right thing. Prayer is that right thing; it's where we should start. Prayer—praising God for his attributes and calling out to him with his covenant promises in mind—is essential and necessary for creating a culture of evangelism. God's sovereignty and our responsibility are intended to work together to rid us of both anxiety and apathy. This right understanding is fleshed out when we practice prayer as a church.

J. I. Packer states the two great obstacles to salvation: "man's natural and irresistible impulse to oppose God, and . . . Satan's assiduity in shepherding man in the ways of unbelief and disobedience."[4] We become more aware of our inadequacy when we recognize that people are unable to turn to God naturally. This leads us to the conclusion that "the sovereignty of God in grace gives us our only hope of success in evangelism."[5] The only hope we have is that God is in control. Meditation on God's sovereignty is the medication that calms our anxious hearts. When rightly applied to our hopes for success, our labor is more energized as God's sovereignty becomes the engine behind our efforts.

The antidote for carrying weight we were never meant to carry is to let someone else carry it for us. Many of our evangelistic efforts are driven solely by pragmatism and strategy, when lasting, abiding fruit comes from prayer (see John 15:8, 16). Praying together removes the pressure for "success" and puts it back on God's shoulders. When we pray, "Our Father in heaven," we acknowledge God is sovereign and does what he pleases. When we pray for God to save someone, we admit that God alone has the power to do so. When we thank him for our salvation, it's because we know he saved us—we didn't save ourselves. As we pray to God for salvation, we realize that God's sovereignty diminishes only our anxiety and apathy, not our activity. Prayer, then, is the pump at the gas station that connects us to the fuel for faithful evangelism.

But before we're mobilized for mission, we must know what evangelism is. Evangelism is proclaiming the gospel message and inviting sinners to respond. While we must be careful to clarify God's work in evangelism, we must also properly understand our own. When we evangelize, we place sin in the context of a wrong relationship with God, lest nonbelievers think of sin as something other than breaking a holy God's law. We must ensure that sin isn't seen as a generic attitude, but is equated with specific actions of which we must repent. Lastly, sin must be understood as something that corrupts our very nature as God's image bearers. Understanding sin in this way helps us see that we don't have the ability to simply change our actions. We need a Savior to provide us a new heart.

If God has given us a task with results that aren't dependent on us, then it's erroneous to define evangelism by its results. Successful evangelism isn't measured by the end result, but by our faithfulness to the task. We seek to faithfully instruct people in the gospel and freely invite them to take God at his word—promised forgiveness for genuine repentance. This faithful proclamation should provide us rest. We can take a deep breath as we pray for God to do what only he can do, and to help us do what he's called us to do. Praying together fills us with concern for the lost. Since God is the one doing the heavy lifting of salvation, we can be concerned for others without being crushed by the weight of that entire burden falling on us.

By gathering to pray, we keep our concern for the lost fresh inside of us. Spurgeon shows us the importance of this in his book *The Soul Winner*:

> While this is how things should be, what do we see in many places? Nobody prays much about the matter, no meetings are called for crying to God for a blessing, and the minister never encourages the people to come and tell him about the work of grace in their souls. I tell you this, he has his reward. He gets what he asked for and receives what he expected. His Master gives him his penny but nothing else. The command is, Open thy mouth wide, and I will fill it (Psalm 81:10). Yet, here we sit with closed lips waiting for the blessing. Open your mouth with a full expectation, a firm belief, and according to your faith so shall it be unto you.[6]

A REMEDY THAT REPLACES

Praying together does something wonderful to our evangelism. It doesn't just erase the obstacles to evangelism; it replaces them. Anxiety is replaced with boldness. Apathy is replaced with compassion. Our liabilities are turned into assets for gospel advancement in the world.

We need courage. We all have things to be afraid of. We lack the strength, sufficiency, and wisdom that would guarantee our safety. We're scared of being overcome and outsmarted. We're afraid of failing, and rightly so. We have all the ingredients for failure. But thankfully, God doesn't have this fear. No one can threaten him. He has the courage we so desperately need. And here's even better news: he is on our side. Like the scrawny kid with a strong older brother who's ready to fight a bully stronger than him, we get courage through prayer because prayer connects us to the power of God. Notice that in the Gospels, the rash, prideful, and cowering Peter isn't characterized by prayer. But, as we saw in the last chapter, in the book of Acts, he's constantly praying, and thus constantly bold and faithful to proclaim the gospel.

Prayer replaces apathy with compassion. When we thank God for our salvation, we're reminded it isn't an achievement we should scold people for not attaining; rather, it's a gift we should pity them for not taking hold of. Through prayer, Jonah's question of, "What will happen to me if I go?" is quickly replaced with, "What will happen to *them* if I stay?" Through prayer, we find out that it's impossible to pray for people and hold on to bitterness or indifference toward them. We're connected to the heart of God as we pray for the salvation of souls.

ENCOURAGING EVANGELISM IN THE LOCAL CHURCH

We must regularly reinforce this connection between God's sovereignty and our responsibility by frequently praying for conversions as a church and thanking God for them. Packer writes, "Whatever side you may have taken in debates on this question in the past, in your heart you believe in the sovereignty of God no less firmly than anyone else. On our feet we may have arguments about it, but on our knees we are all agreed."[7] Constantly affirming God's sovereignty and our responsibility in evangelism in prayer helps the church believe and live this out, even if we can't perfectly articulate it. Making prayers for conversion a staple of our time together will go a long way in creating a culture of evangelism.

We must also highlight the role of prayer in our preaching. Romans 9, a chapter on God's sovereignty, is followed by Romans 10, a chapter on our responsibility. In between this investigation of God's sovereignty and the instruction to evangelize, the apostle Paul prays for conversions (Rom. 10:1–4). Consistent, articulate, and careful gospel preaching week after week familiarizes the congregation with hearing and understanding the gospel. Similarly, highlighting the role of prayer helps them understand the vital part they play in God's kingdom. We'll see their confidence in the gospel and prayer increase, along with their competence in communicating the gospel to nonbelievers.

Where do missionaries come from? Jesus seems to think they come as a result of God responding to our prayers: "The harvest is plentiful, but the laborers are few. Therefore pray earnestly to the Lord of the harvest to send out laborers into his harvest" (Luke 10:2). By praying for laborers, God raises up gospel workers and reminds those of us who are inactive that it starts with us. Praying for success in evangelism is a prayer for gospel laborers. It's crucial to link the two in the minds of our church members.

We should also constantly keep the needs of any supported workers sent from our body in the forefront, because we want the members of our church to know that they carry the burden of participating in God's saving work through prayer.

God's evangelistic strategy in the world is rooted in the local church. The local church gives a watching world a firsthand encounter of the love, forgiveness, mercy, and holiness of God. This is why we pray for other churches and pastors in our area during our gatherings. We pray that God would cause these churches to thrive for his glory, and that people would hear the gospel through them. We pray that God would raise up other pastors to continue this faithful gospel work—both locally and abroad.

By praying together for repentance in our lives and in the lives of those who don't yet know Christ, we don't just do something with our discontentment. We do the right thing: we pray.

CONCLUSION

Fighting Temptations

Are you convinced yet? Prayer is a bigger deal than we've made it out to be. It's vital for the life of our churches. I hope this short resource will make a difference in the way your church prays and experiences God's faithfulness through prayer.

Having read books on prayer before, I know the difficulty isn't in starting to pray more. The difficulty is in sustaining this attitude. It's not hard to start. It's hard to solidify habits.

Over the years, I've learned that I don't need to send out a survey or do market research on people's common temptations. I merely need to look inside my own heart and see where I've failed to pray.

So here's a list of temptations common to all of us when it comes to practicing prayer in the life of the church. Much of what is listed below has been stated throughout the book, so think of this as the inventory of what's been placed on the shelf over the course of these pages. I want to reinforce these realities so the way forward will be clear.

The first step in fighting temptations is exposing and naming them. Therefore, I will attempt to be as candid as I am concise. The next step involves getting back on track. So I'll attempt to point you back to the track. Let's throw some paint on this invisible enemy of ours so we don't get blindsided. We're not ignorant of his schemes, so let's expose them for what they are.

Temptation 1: Cancel a prayer meeting.

Something will come up. Something always comes up. God gives us the gift of being able to communicate with him anytime and anywhere. You'd think that kind of accessibility would make us fervent in prayer, but it doesn't. It makes us flexible in a bad way, always assuming we can make time for it later. If there's anything I've learned from over twenty years in school as a professional procrastinator, it is that later never comes as soon as you thought it would.

Track to run on: Don't postpone the priority of prayer. As best you can, treat corporate prayer times as cemented and fixed. The first time you cancel a prayer meeting (or miss one) isn't that big of a deal. But the second, third, and fourth times begin to say something about prayer's priority in your church life. We aren't given the freedom of communication with God to neatly fit it around our schedules. We're given this free and frequent access to God because we're always in need of it. Therefore, we should always pray (see 1 Thess. 5:17).

You help cement this truth in the life of your church by your persistence in prayer and your presence when your church prays. I don't imagine that many of us struggle with praying too much, or that other priorities fall through the cracks because we attend too many prayer meetings. So I'll just end this here. Pastor, don't cancel prayer meetings. Christian, don't miss them.

Temptation 2: Form your theology of prayer around how God has answered your most recent prayer.

How often have we been discouraged when God says, "No"? Quitting usually begins here. Why bother praying when prayer doesn't work? "I earnestly, consistently, and faithfully prayed for a loved one's healing, and he still passed away. I'm through praying."

Track to run on: Keep track of the things you've prayed for. Every one of them. Pastor, this is how you can help your church persevere. Christian, this is where you can help your church maintain faithfulness. Routinely revisiting the list of things you've prayed for can help you see just how faithful God has actually been, even in ways you've completely forgotten. By doing this you leave a trail of breadcrumbs for your church to recount the faithfulness of God when they feel like they're in the wilderness.

Sometimes in the life of a church unanswered prayers are just as helpful as answered ones. They remind us that we aren't imposing our will on God. He's in control. We're making requests, but they're just that: requests, not demands. He has a better view of things than we do, so we thank him in hindsight for every prayer answered or left unanswered. Prayer is leaving the direction of our lives in God's hands. Nine years of praying for kids made the adoption of our baby daughter all the more sweet, especially as we shared what God had done. Through this experience we saw hundreds (if not thousands) of people who journeyed with us over the years rejoice in God's faithfulness.

In 2015, on the Sunday evening that we constituted as a church in the midst of one of our darkest seasons together, we began our time by reading a list of the twenty-five things that we had constantly prayed for over the previous eight months in regard to the success of the church and establishing a gospel witness in Atlanta's West End. We then read the twenty-five ways that God exceeded every expectation. Our goal was not to teach that God gives us everything we ask for, if we ask hard enough. It was to highlight God's faithfulness in seasons of suffering because it's easy for us to forget. It's like the penny that blocks the sun because it's too close to someone's eyes. Keep track of God's faithfulness, and help your church remove the penny from time to time.

Temptation 3: Individualize what God has meant to be corporate.

Just because we can pray privately doesn't mean that we must only pray privately. Though prayer is often an individual task, we should regularly and routinely involve others. If we struggle to pray, the tendency is to hide.

Track to run on: Don't shy away from using plural pronouns in your prayers, especially in corporate gatherings. Using plural pronouns in corporate gatherings reminds the church that we are participants and not merely spectators when we gather. Using plural pronouns in private prayer helps to remind us we're not merely individuals but also part of a family. Names, faces, and smiles, not merely silhouettes, should come to mind when we think of "us." This is the beauty of joining a local church. Those silhouettes are filled with specific people and their specific needs.

Praying together, even while confessing sin, is God's recipe for experiencing freedom. It humbles us. That's why James writes that we should confess our sin to each other and pray for each other that we may be healed (see James 5:16). My good friend John Henderson says the reason God tells us to confess to each other is because what keeps us from confessing our sin is the very thing keeping us trapped in that sin (i.e., pride, fear of man, ego). Those are the sins that lie underneath the surface. Involving others in our prayers, especially those of confession, is God's great gift of freedom to us.

Temptation 4: Assume people know what prayer is and how they should do it.

This is the drum I've been beating for the past one hundred pages. Just because prayer is necessary doesn't mean it comes naturally to us.

Track to run on: Don't miss an opportunity to instruct others to pray. While you may be an excellent pray-er who doesn't require much preparation before leading public prayers, please know that extemporaneous prayers may not provide the best examples for others to follow. Again, I'm not telling you to craft prayers and perform them. I'm telling you to prepare beforehand so that the rest of the church is edified and your prayer becomes an example for them.

When it comes to singing, everybody wants a composed

song. But when it comes to prayer, many insist on improvisation. Preparing prayers beforehand isn't the enemy of authenticity. It's an ally of clarity and an expression of love, not just for God but for others. Writing prayers beforehand and offering them up to God in the presence of his people isn't any less authentic than writing a letter to your wife and giving it to her the next day. The words of the letter are heartfelt. She might even be more appreciative that you took the time to clarify your thoughts and put them down on paper. Preparation is a helpful way to communicate your heart clearly.

We don't just instruct people propositionally, but practically. Learn to incorporate the question, "How can I pray for you?" whenever you hear a problem or concern. Let problems, concerns, or even furrowed brows become a trigger for you to ask this question. Since we can pray to God anytime, don't put off fulfilling the request. Do it on the spot, and you'll help others learn prayer's usefulness. Children learn what a dog is by watching someone point one out to them when it walks by, not by looking up the word *dog* in the dictionary. They learn in the context of real life. Prayer works the same way. Reading a book on prayer is fine. Releasing your burdens to each other and together taking them to God is better.

Temptation 5: Measure the effectiveness of your prayer gathering by the amount of people that attend.

This temptation, especially in our results-oriented culture, is one of the most difficult ones to move past. If you find yourself struggling for months or years with only a few people attending prayer meetings, it's easy to think you're doing something wrong. You'll be tempted to think you need to innovate.

Track to run on: Think intentionality, not innovation. The best way that I know how to be intentional is to pray about everything. Let the temptation to worry serve as the divine alarm clock reminding you it's time to pray. You have plenty of these coming at you all day. Don't wait until the prayer meeting to pray with others. Sometimes it's the consistent, passionate, and repeated prayers outside the prayer meeting that serve as the lighter fluid to get our cold hearts warm enough to pray with others.

Also, prepare to be disappointed. The prayer gathering will likely have poor attendance, at least initially. But keep fighting. If you have only one other person, it's a prayer meeting. Don't be so quick to give up or to assume something needs to change. Something may need to change, or you may just need to keep being faithful. Be obedient to what God has called us to do as a church, and sow those seeds. God will give the increase in due time.

Cultivating prayer in the life of the church is a marathon, not a sprint. It's like the process of an acorn becoming an oak tree. It takes a long time and lots of ordinary work that isn't recognized or acknowledged. Many external elements work against its cultivation in the life of the church—none more apparent than prosperity.

Prayer often thrives where persecution exists. The absence of hard times cultivates a sense of self-sufficiency that leads us to believe we have all we need. Don't give up. Remind the church of their desperate need for God, and then do all that you can to take them right to his front doorstep through prayer. Prepare to not have a massive following initially. Be okay with that. The power of our prayers isn't found in the number of people praying, but the willingness of the One to whom we're praying.

THE SHELF LIFE

Prayer, as taught by Jesus in the Lord's Prayer, is a perishable item. Don't think of his template as a canned good that's meant to last throughout all eternity. Rather, think of it as a fresh loaf of bread with a shelf life. I'm talking about real bread, not those fast-food buns that will make their way into the eschaton because they never expire. Prayer's usefulness is intended for this life. On the new earth we won't need to pray the way we've been instructed to here—calling on God to fulfill his promises to us. In eternity we will revel in his faithfulness; we will no longer need to *request* that he come quickly and fulfill his promises to us. The Bible ends not with a prayer, but a blessing. Revelation 20:20 is praying for the Lord to come quickly, and then verse 21 follows with a pronouncement of blessing and grace on those of us who are waiting for him.

"Our Father in heaven, hallowed be your name" (Matt. 6:9). We will thank him for this reality *forever*, but we will have no reason to offer up this prayer as a *request*. God will dwell with us! Heaven will meet earth, and his name will be honored by everyone throughout all eternity.

"Your kingdom come. Your will be done, on earth as it is in heaven" (Matt. 6:10). This will already have been accomplished. Not in an already-but-not-yet sense, but in an already, completely, and fully done sense. There will be no need to wait on a later prophecy. There will be no more enemies attempting to overthrow his kingdom. We'll rejoice that this has already happened. We won't need to make a request for it to take place.

"Give us this day our daily bread" (Matt. 6:11). We'll be face-to-face forever with the Bread of Life.

"And forgive us our debts, as we also have forgiven our debtors" (Matt. 6:12). We'll have experienced the culmination of this truth with no need for Jesus to forgive any more of our sins. We'll be living in that forgiveness with no ongoing need to forgive others because everyone will be made perfect. Our capacity for sin will be completely removed.

"And lead us not into temptation, but deliver us from evil" (Matt. 6:13). Satan will be spending eternity in the place of eternal torment prepared for him, while we'll be safely in the home prepared for us by our loving Father. There will be an infinite separation between us and the enemy of our souls. He will have no access to us.

All of the *requests* in the Lord's Prayer will be unnecessary in heaven. God will have already provided everything we need. We'll need only to spend the rest of eternity thanking him.

When Christ teaches us how to pray, he does so with a fractured world in mind. Like manna created for consumption that same day, prayer (in the way we've discussed it here: God's people calling out to God to fulfill his covenant promises) has a shelf life. Its usefulness doesn't extend into the tomorrow that is eternity. So don't wait until tomorrow to make use of it. You have today. You have breath in your lungs right now. So breathe deeply, breathe often, and breathe together.

NOTES

Introduction

1. John Stott in *Ten Great Preachers*, ed. Bill Turpie (Grand Rapids, MI: Baker, 2000), 117.

Chapter 1: Breathe Again: The Problem of Prayerlessness

1. Google's test of omniscience fails here. Apparently only God knows where this quote originated. Some say Martin Luther, others say Martin Luther King Jr. Seeing as to how MLK was named after Martin Luther, let's just attribute this to both of them.

2. E. M. Bounds, *E. M. Bounds on Prayer* (Peabody, MA: Hendrickson, 2006), 118.

Chapter 2: A Class Act: Teach Us to Pray

1. James R. Estep Jr., Michael J. Anthony, and Gregg R. Allison, *A Theology for Christian Education* (Nashville: B&H, 2008), 6.

2. Gary Millar, *Calling on the Name of the Lord: A Biblical Theology of Prayer, New Studies in Biblical Theology* (Downers Grove, IL: InterVarsity Press, 2016), 27.

3. Millar, *Calling*, 26.

4. Millar, *Calling*, 27.

5. John Calvin in Millar, *Calling*, 15–16.

6. Mark Dever, *What Is a Healthy Church?* (Wheaton, IL: Crossway, 2007), 26.

Chapter 3: The World Is Yours: A Family Led

1. J. C. Ryle, *A Call to Prayer: With Study Guide* (Pensacola, FL: Chapel Library, 1998), 35, Kindle.

2. J. I. Packer expounds on this in greater depth in his chapter "Sons of God," in *Knowing God* (1973; repr., Downers Grove, IL: InterVarsity Press, 1993).

3. Packer, *Knowing God*, 201.

4. A. W. Tozer, *Prayer* (Chicago: Moody, 2016), 175.

Chapter 4: Soul Food: A Family Fed

1. J. C. Ryle, *A Call to Prayer: With Study Guide* (Pensacola, FL: Chapel Library, 1998), 34, Kindle.

2. Ryle, *A Call to Prayer*, 34–35.

Chapter 5: Roots: A Family Bred

1. C. S. Lewis, *A Grief Observed* (1961; repr., New York: Bantam, 1976), 61.

2. J. C. Ryle, *A Call to Prayer: With Study Guide* (Pensacola, FL: Chapel Library, 1998), 11, Kindle.

3. Sir Arthur Conan Doyle, *The Greatest Adventures of Sherlock Holmes* (New York: Fall River Press, 2012), 151.

4. Thank you to James Allman, Dallas Theological Seminary.

Chapter 7: Lean on Me: The Role of Prayer in Corporate Care

1. Charles H. Spurgeon, *The Soul Winner (Updated Edition): How to Lead Sinners to the Saviour* (Abbotsford, WI: Aneko Press, 2016), 84.

Chapter 8: Doing the Right Thing: The Role of Prayer in Missions

1. Blake Morgan, "Netflix and Late Fees: How Consumer-Centric Companies Are Changing the Tide," *Forbes.com*, October 7, 2016, https://www.forbes.com/sites/blakemorgan/2016/10/07/netflix-late-fees-and-consumer-centric-ideas.

2. Gina Keating, "Five Myths about Netflix," *The Washington Post* online, February 21, 2014, https://www.washingtonpost.com/opinions/five-myths-about-netflix/2014/02/21/787c7c8e-9a3f-11e3-b931-0204122c514b_story.html.

3. Mark Dever, "Closed Mouths Lead to an Open Hell" (sermon, Capitol Hill Baptist Church, Washington, D.C., November 24, 2013).

4. J. I. Packer, *Evangelism and the Sovereignty of God* (1961; repr., Downers Grove, IL: InterVarsity Press, 2008), 106.

5. Packer, *Evangelism*, 105.

6. Charles H. Spurgeon, *The Soul Winner (Updated Edition), How to Lead Sinners to the Saviour* (Abbotsford, WI: Aneko Press, 2016), 38.

7. Packer, *Evangelism*, 21.

GENERAL INDEX

SCRIPTURE INDEX

IX 9Marks

Building Healthy Churches

9Marks exists to equip church leaders with a biblical vision and practical resources for displaying God's glory to the nations through healthy churches.

To that end, we want to see churches characterized by these nine marks of health:

1   Expositional Preaching
2   Biblical Theology
3   A Biblical Understanding of the Gospel
4   A Biblical Understanding of Conversion
5   A Biblical Understanding of Evangelism
6   Biblical Church Membership
7   Biblical Church Discipline
8   Biblical Discipleship
9   Biblical Church Leadership

Find all our Crossway titles
and other resources at
www.9Marks.org

9MARKS: BUILDING HEALTHY CHURCHES SERIES

Based on Mark Dever's best-selling book *Nine Marks of a Healthy Church*, each book in this series helps readers grasp basic biblical commands regarding the local church.

TITLES INCLUDE:

Biblical Theology	Conversion	The Gospel
Church Discipline	Discipling	Missions
Church Elders	Evangelism	Prayer
Church Membership	Expositional Preaching	Sound Doctrine

For more information, visit crossway.org.
For translated versions of these and other 9Marks books, visit 9Marks.org/bookstore/translations.